THE PSYCHIC ENERGY WORKBOOK

A graduated course in psychic skills based on the fundamental awareness of how we can use the psychic energy we all possess.

THE
PSYCHIC ENERGY
WORKBOOK

An Illustrated Course in Practical Psychic Skills

by

R. MICHAEL MILLER and JOSEPHINE M. HARPER

Edited by Jo C. Harper

Photography by James F. Lowell
Photographs illustrated by Robert Boustany

THE AQUARIAN PRESS
Wellingborough, Northamptonshire

First published 1986

British Library Cataloguing in Publication Data

Miller, R. Michael
The psychic energy workbook: an
illustrated course in practical psychic skills.
1. Psychical research
I. Title   II. Harper, Josephine M.
133.8   BF1031

ISBN 0-85030-529-2

The Aquarian Press is part of the Thorsons Publishing Group, Wellingborough, Northamptonshire, NN8 2RQ, England

Printed in Great Britain by Woolnough Bookbinding Limited, Irthlingborough, Northamptonshire

5   7   9   10   8   6   4

ACKNOWLEDGEMENTS

In any endeavour of this kind, a great deal of help is needed from many people. Our students' comments and participation have been important to us. In addition, we are most grateful to our editor Jo Carolyn Harper who helped bring it all together.

CONTENTS

INTRODUCTION

Psychic events and abilities are part of our human heritage. We are all psychic. For some of us the abilities lie dormant, but most of us use them daily without recognizing them. Often we do not see our hunches and perceptions for what they are, nor do we understand their relationship to the spectacular abilities demonstrated by some psychics. Our aim at the Psychic Studies Institute is to track the physical basis of such events. Our research indicates that they happen via a physical substance that is produced in the body. We refer to this substance as psychic energy. The same substance is called 'prana' by yogis, 'chi' by practitioners of the martial arts, and 'bio-energy' by therapists.

Psychic energy is generated by all living things and is transferred between them. This transferral forms the basis for all psychic events and is part of all human communication. Psychic energy is a physical substance – a flexible medium which is light and diffuse, but which can be compacted and moulded so as to be readily perceptible by the physical senses. It is our use of psychic energy – this substance that is present in all life – which makes us psychic creatures. Conscious perception and control of psychic energy are essential to the development of conscious psychic skill.

To become aware of our psychic abilities and to improve them is largely a matter of learning to use psychic energy with awareness and skill. Such skill is acquired only with careful, consistent practice. Any human talent, whether in mathematics, music, or psychic work, must be trained and cultivated in order to reach its full potential.

The students at the Psychic Studies Institute tell us that developing their psychic abilities has benefited them in their work and in their other daily activities. Indeed, it is our feeling that psychic skills should be natural and easy, serving to make life smoother and integrating with ordinary interactions. To this end, we have designed a course to help you verify for yourself that psychic energy does exist, that it is physical, and that psychic skills can be of practical benefit to you.

The exercises in this book are designed for two or more people. Working with a partner allows you to get feedback. As you practise the exercises, you will learn how well your energy-body can produce effects, and you will observe your partner's improvement. The exercises follow a progression. By using this sequence and following the daily training, you will develop the energy-body strength necessary for the advanced work. Chapter 7 contains additional exercises designed for those people fortunate enough to have several friends who are interested in working together. The exercises in Chapter 7 form a gradual progression from elementary to advanced psychic work.

As you work with these exercises and develop psychic skills, it is important that you write down what you have done and what your results are. Keeping a journal is an integral part of this course. Often the things you accomplish will later seem nebulous and unclear. By keeping a journal, you can accurately evaluate your progress.

It is important also that you maintain an open mind as you work. If you feel strongly that you cannot perceive energy, or if you believe that psychic skills are nonsense, you will be likely to close off any perception that you might have. We urge you to be open to possibilities, but also to be judicious and objective in the interpretation of your experiences. Your journal will be an important element in the objective evaluation of your progress.

You are affected by your own psychic energy, by other people's psychic energy, and by the psychic energy of your environment. Psychic energy is transferred from one person to another and among all living things. All of us constantly exchange energy with each other and with nature. We are profoundly affected by this fundamental exchange, although it seems very subtle. For us to become aware of the energies that surround us is like a fish becoming aware of the water he swims in. It is a basic, but unobserved, reality.

As you master basic psychic skills, you will find that energy vibrates to different frequencies, carrying emotions and other information. In addition, you will find that each person's energy is composed of a range of frequencies that make up his unique vibration. Sometimes the various frequencies of energy with which we come in contact are distracting or are incompatible with our own. Psychic cleaning is, therefore, an important part of the course and an important element in clear, reliable perception. This perception and sensitivity can be enhanced further without increasing your vulnerability, through the use of self-defence techniques.

In this course you will also learn consciously to perceive information carried on psychic energy. Energy with information on it can be contained in physical objects such as jewellery. You will learn to read and interpret such information from objects, as well as to read and interpret information gathered through energy rapport with other people. You will find that such rapport supplies information, facilitates communication, and harmonizes groups.

As you and your partner work with the exercises in this book, you will develop your psychic strength and will increase your control and perception of psychic energy. You will find the areas in which your psychic talents lie, and you will also discover and strengthen your weak areas. We believe that you will enjoy practising these exercises and will find them beneficial.

Points to keep in mind throughout this book:
   All living things have psychic energy.
   Psychic energy is a physical substance.
   Psychic energy is exchanged in all human communications.

Sending and perceiving energy.

Chapter 1

FUNDAMENTALS OF PSYCHIC ENERGY

As you practise the exercises in this chapter, you will develop your perception of psychic energy. You will also develop your ability to direct psychic energy with precision, and you will develop your psychic strength. You will begin by learning to perceive kinaesthetically – by touch. You will learn to feel energy entering and leaving your body as your partner directs it to you. Precision in the placement and direction of energy is essential for psychic work. You will begin your development of precision by learning to direct a clear, strong, steady beam of energy to your partner. You will also learn to utilize your full psychic strength through psychic calisthenics and grounded positions.

EXERCISE 1.   EXCHANGING ENERGY

Repetitions   Six or more.

Preparation   Read the entire exercise before you begin. Wear natural-fibre clothing and no jewellery (see Appendix). For this and most other experiments, you and your partner will need a dish of rock salt. Sit opposite your partner. One of you will be the Perceiver, the other the Sender, of energy. Then you will exchange roles.

Explanation   In this exercise, you will be learning to perceive and direct the physical energy that is the basis for all psychic events. You will learn to direct your energy and to perceive energy directed to you. As you work with these skills, keep in mind that you are working with a physical substance and that you are using a part of your physical body to direct it. Some people find this surprising since psychic energy is not readily visible, but many of the things that make up our physical world are invisible – electricity, for example. Like electricity, a sufficient quantity of psychic energy must be gathered and directed in the proper way before it can be readily perceived.

Perceiver's Instructions   Allow yourself to be open to your partner's psychic energy. Your frame of mind is important. Your clear intention must be to

Exercise 1.1   Generating energy.

receive energy. Be sure that your arms are relaxed and resting on the table or on your legs so that you are not confused by sensations of muscular tension or a change in blood flow. You will experience a gentle sensation in your hand as your partner directs energy into it. Our students have described the sensation variously as feeling warm or cool, as tingling, or as resembling static electricity.

Exercise 1.2   Preparing to send energy.

Each person's psychic perceptions are a little different, especially in the beginning. One of the interesting things about this course is learning in what way your perception functions, so that you can make reliable use of it.

Sender's Instructions   Visualize your body surrounded by light. Absorb this light-energy into all parts of your body except your head. You may want to visualize yourself as a sponge, absorbing light-energy throughout your body. Now, using this energy, form a globe just beneath your navel in the centre of your body. Be aware of this light-energy growing more and more intense.

Feel the energy flowing up your chest and over to your right arm. Close your right hand, thumb inside the fingers. Let the energy flow down your arm and build up in your right hand. Visualize the energy growing and glowing in your hand, completely contained within you.

When you feel ready, move your extended index finger to a point about one inch from the tip of your partner's index finger and let your built-up energy flow into his finger. If you move too close, he may be confused by your body heat; if your finger is too far away from his, the energy may be diffused.

Maintain this energy flow for a few seconds, until your partner clearly perceives the energy. You may need to pause and build up energy again. Then direct the energy to different areas of your partner's hand. Some areas are likely to be more perceptive than others.

Conclusion Change roles and repeat. Record your observations in your journal.

Trouble-shooting After you have exchanged energy a few times, either or both of you may find that you have too much energy in your hands. If this happens, you may feel a heavy, full, tingling sensation. It may even happen that your hands become swollen or red. To remove the excess energy, scrape it into the bowl of rock salt which will absorb it. Clearly visualize the energy being cleaned from your hands. If your hands are swollen, gently direct energy out of your fingers and palms into the rock salt (see Appendix).

If you become lightheaded when doing these exercises, it is probable that excess energy has gathered in your head. Overloading the delicate channels in the head decreases perception and control. At such times, it is necessary consciously to draw the energy into the lower parts of your body. To do this, visualize the energy flowing down from your head and into your feet. You may wish to get up and walk around for a few minutes. Do not do any psychic work while you are lightheaded (see Appendix).

Your psychic development is most likely to progress in the same ways that your development in other areas has. Listen to yourself. Just as it is possible to strain your muscles when doing a new exercise, so it is possible to strain your energy-body. If you begin to feel tired, stop and rest. Pushing yourself too quickly through the exercises will only end in slowing your progress, just as it would if you were building physical muscles. Equally, if you are having a slow start, keep in mind that patient persistence will be rewarded as it is with any skill. In many ways talent is less important than discipline. Soon your psychic work will be easy and exhilarating.

Variation After you have practised this exercise six or more times and feel confident of your ability to send and perceive energy, you may want to experiment and see if you are more perceptive in some areas than others. The Perceiver will close his eyes and the Sender will direct energy to different areas of the Perceiver's body. Can you perceive energy with your lips, or your forehead, or your back?

EXERCISE 2.   TAKING ENERGY

Repetitions   Six or more.

Preparation   Read the entire exercise. Wear natural-fibre clothing and no jewellery. Have the rock salt ready so you can clean the excess energy off your hands as necessary. Sit opposite your partner.

Explanation   In the first exercise you gave and received energy. This time the Sender will first give energy and then will actively pull it back. Energy interchange is one of our most basic forms of communication. Focusing on this directed method will help awaken your perception of energy interchange in other areas of your life.

Perceiver's Instructions   As before, you will want to be attentive, relaxed and receptive. By now you are familiar with your partner's energy. Be alert for the difference in sensation as your partner gives energy to you, then takes it from you. Give your partner feedback.

Our students generally find that as the hand fills with energy, it feels fuller or heavier, and that this sensation reverses as the energy leaves. Practise until you are able clearly to distinguish between energy being given to you and energy being taken from you. Clean your hands periodically to make perception easier. Allow yourself to be acted upon and relax, focusing on your psychic perception. You may wish to close your eyes; some of our students find that focusing on only one sense helps make perception easier.

Sender's Instructions   Form a bright globe in the centre of your body and generate energy as you did in the first experiment. Send the energy in the same way as before. Because your partner is learning what to look for and is attempting to develop his perception, tell him each time you begin and each time you finish giving energy.

Now prepare to draw the energy back. Place your hand in the same position as before, visualizing a small tube between your finger and your partner's finger. Visualize the energy moving from your partner's hand into yours. You may want to visualize it as air sucked into a vacuum cleaner hose, or as iron filings drawn to a magnet in your hand. Some of our students who are nurses have visualized this process as taking blood with a pipette. Whatever image is clearest and most appealing to you will give the clearest instructions to your energy-body. Alternate between giving and taking energy. Make each giving and taking a separate event, keeping your partner informed as you go.

Conclusion   Change roles and repeat. Were you aware of the energy as it left your body? As it entered your body? Did you notice the difference in sensation between giving energy and taking it? Were you able to keep your hand relaxed? Muscular tension can interfere with energy flow and perception. Record your observations in your journal.

Trouble-shooting   Sometimes it happens that the Perceiver is able to feel energy flow, but is unsure of its direction. Accurate perception will come with practice.

As in Exercise 1, you may feel that too much energy is building up in your hands. If so, scrape the excess energy into the bowl of rock salt. If you feel lightheaded, draw the excess energy down into the lower parts of your body; get up and walk around for a few minutes before continuing your psychic work.

EXERCISE 3.   TESTING PERCEPTION OF ENERGY FLOW

Repetitions   Six or more.

Preparation   Read the entire exercise. Wear natural-fibre clothing and no jewellery. Have the rock salt ready. Sit opposite your partner.

Explanation   Now you are probably eager to see how accurately you are perceiving, how clearly you are sending and how strongly you are taking energy. This exercise is a test you will want to return to many times as it will sharpen your perceptions and build your confidence in them. Only by testing a method can you learn to trust it.

Perceiver's Instructions   Be sure your hands are loose and relaxed. Let yourself be receptive. Clean your hands between each exchange. Write down your perception.

Sender's Instructions   Write down your plan for giving and taking energy. In order to have a fair test, you must be careful that your partner does not see your list. It might look like this:

1.   Give
2.   Take
3.   Take
4.   Give
5.   Take

As before, form a bright globe in the centre of your body, and generate energy. Give or take energy in your chosen order. This is a test of your control as well as of your partner's perception.

Trouble-shooting   The Sender must be careful not to give obvious physical clues. For example, do not inhale deeply or draw your hand back as you take energy; do not move your hand forward as you give energy; do not stare at your partner's hand as you give energy, or stare at your own hand as you take energy.

Conclusion   Compare lists. Change roles and repeat. Record your observations in your journal.

EXERCISE 4. SOLO EXERCISE: GROUNDED POSITIONS (USING YOUR ENTIRE ENERGY-BODY)

Repetitions   Do this exercise before doing any psychic work.

Preparation   Read the entire exercise. Wear natural-fibre clothing and no jewellery.

Explanation   You have been using your energy-body, sometimes referred to as your astral body or body of light, both to direct energy and to perceive it. Although composed entirely of energy, the energy-body has complexities and follows natural laws just as the physical body does. Using the whole energy-body to do any psychic task or exercise makes it possible to accomplish more with less effort.

To use your whole energy-body, it is necessary for you to feel in touch with your whole physical body. This will help you become more grounded and will make more energy available to you.

Instructions, Standing Posture   Stand with your feet about eighteen inches apart. Place your weight forward on the balls of your feet. Flex your knees slightly, and relax your shoulders. Breathe deeply and evenly. Now flex each part of your body gently, beginning with your feet. Lift each foot and rotate each ankle. Become aware of your whole body, paying particular attention to the lower half – the feet, legs, knees, and hips. Focus your attention about two inches below your navel, in the centre of your body. When you feel centred, you are ready to begin your psychic exercises.

Instructions, Sitting Posture   Sit cross-legged on a rug or pillow. Lean forward, arching your back slightly. Relax. Let your arms rest on your knees and thighs. This position is called the tailor posture in yoga. You may substitute the full or the half-lotus posture if either is comfortable for you. Do not strain. The position should be easy: your body should be comfortable and well-balanced so that you are free to concentrate on your psychic activities.

Move your feet and legs slightly. Relax, and increase your awareness of your entire body, especially the legs and feet which we often neglect. Breathe deeply and easily for a minute or two, then focus your awareness in the centre of your body. Now you are ready to do psychic work.

Trouble-shooting   Although none of our students has ever experienced any difficulty as a result of doing this exercise, if you feel discomfort while performing it or any other exercise in this book, stop at once.

Variation   Review the first three exercises using your entire energy-body. Note down any differences in your performance. Perceiver, can you tell a difference in the amount and strength of the energy? Sender, is the exercise becoming easier? Occasionally it takes so much less effort to send energy when grounded that it appears to the Sender that nothing is happening. However, the Perceiver can help by giving feedback. Perceiving energy also becomes easier when the Grounded Positions are used. The Perceiver often feels stronger than before and his perceptions are clearer.

You may enjoy testing the exercise further. Alternate using your whole energy-body and not using it. Record your observations in your journal.

EXERCISE 5. FIELD WORK: USING YOUR ENTIRE ENERGY-BODY DURING CONVERSATION

Repetitions Three or more.

Preparation Read the entire exercise. Wear natural-fibre clothing and no jewellery. You will need someone to converse with who does not realize that he is part of your experiment.

Explanation As you have seen, the use of the entire energy-body makes the transmission of energy easier and more effective. Because of this, using your entire energy-body in daily situations will make you impressive and will make the projection of your ideas more forceful. Use a Grounded Position any time you particularly wish your viewpoint to be heard or felt.

Having practised the Grounded Positions, you are now ready to experiment with their effects in ordinary interactions. You can readily adapt the Grounded Positions for public use. The key is to keep balanced and loose. Be aware of your entire body, and focus on your centre. It is essential not to lock the joints or constrict the muscles. Knees, hips, back, and shoulders should all be loose and mobile to allow the entire power of your energy-body to support you in whatever you do.

Perceiver's Instructions In this exercise you will be a detached observer. You must watch your partner in conversation and note how the person he is talking with reacts. Notice any vocal changes or alteration in body language.

Speaker's Instructions Have your topics ready. Plan in advance to use your energy-body on certain topics and not on others. Make the appropriate energy-body changes as you vary topics in the conversation. To make this a fair test, the Perceiver should not know when you plan to make your changes.

Conclusion Change roles and repeat. Record your observations in your journal. Compare notes.

EXERCISE 6. CALISTHENICS: FLOWING ENERGY THROUGH YOUR ENTIRE BODY

Repetitions Do this exercise daily.

Preparations Read the entire exercise. Wear natural-fibre clothing and no jewellery. Stand in the Grounded Position.

Explanation This exercise is designed to help remove energy blocks and to develop the entire energy-body.

Instructions Using your whole energy-body, build up energy as you did in Exercises 1 and 2. Gather the energy in your right arm. Hold your right hand straight out in front of you, tucking your thumb under; you will not direct energy out of your thumb. Very gently and evenly, push energy out of all four fingers. Maintain the flow for about five seconds. Then take the energy back into your hand and up your forearm. Repeat this three times. Now let the energy flow back into the centre of your body, then up and over into your left arm. Direct the energy evenly out of the four fingers of your left hand. Take the energy back into your body.

  Now draw the energy down your right leg and out of your right foot so that it flows evenly out of all five toes. Bring the energy back in through your toes, up your leg, and into the energy ball in the centre of your body. Do this three times on each side.

Conclusion Record your observations in your journal.

Exercise 6.1 Calisthenics: Flowing energy through your fingertips.

Exercise 6.2 Flowing energy through your entire body.

Trouble-shooting You may experience difficulty in getting energy to flow through some parts of your body. Such difficulty probably indicates the presence of congested energy or an energy block. You should draw energy specifically through the blocked area using a sustained but gentle pressure. This will loosen the block and the congested energy will flow out.

Variation Repeat the above exercise, working with each finger and each toe separately. You may find it easier to send energy out of some fingers than others. If so, this indicates that you have an energy block. Continue to exercise the blocked fingers gently.

EXERCISE 7. SOLO EXERCISE: INCREASING YOUR ENERGY

Repetitions As needed.

Preparations Read the entire exercise. Wear natural-fibre clothing and no jewellery. Stand in the Grounded Position or lie on the grass.

Explanation Free-flowing energy is the key to vitality. Sometimes when we are tired, it is because we lack psychic energy. Since psychic energy is always available from the atmosphere and from all life around us, it is easy to obtain enough energy. This exercise is to be done outside in a pleasant environment – near water, trees, or on the grass.

Instructions Get a sense of your whole body. Are your neck and shoulders tense? Loosen them. Shake your hands and feet a little. Rotate your ankles. Relax. Breathe slowly and evenly. You may want to close your eyes. Absorb energy from the environment around you. Draw it gently and evenly through your entire body. You may wish to use a symbolic image to aid your absorption.

Conclusion   Record your observations in your journal.

Trouble-shooting   If you are wearing synthetic clothing the benefits of the exercise will be lessened. If you are wearing nylon stockings, do not attempt to draw in energy through your feet. Take it in through some other part of your body. It is very helpful to touch a plant or tree.

Urban Variation   It may be difficult to find a natural environment. However, even if you work in an office you can find at least a patch of grass and can slip your shoes off and stand in it barefoot. Then become aware of your whole body and shake loose the tense areas. Stand in the Grounded Position. Keep your knees slightly flexed and your hips loose, so that the energy can flow up your legs to your torso. See the energy, like white light, flowing up your body. Feel it filling your torso and arms. Stop when you are pleasantly charged. If you feel you have taken in more energy than is comfortable, let the excess drain out of your feet.

EXERCISE 8.   SOLO EXERCISE: EXCHANGING ENERGY WITH NATURE

Repetitions   As needed.

Preparation   Read the entire exercise. Wear natural-fibre clothing and no jewellery. Find a large healthy tree. Stand in the Grounded Position with your feet bare.

Explanation   The energy emanating from plants and trees is clean and wholesome. You will find absorbing it beneficial. To draw energy from a tree will not harm the tree. In fact, exchanging energy with nature is part of the same natural cycle as the oxygen and carbon dioxide exchange. You nourish the tree as it nourishes you.

Instructions   Stand barefoot with your back next to the tree. Touch the tree with your palms. Be sure your knees are slightly flexed and your hips are relaxed. Breathe fully and evenly.

Now gently draw in energy from the tree through your hands, arms and back, as you drew it from your partner in Exercise 2. If you want to draw a small amount of energy into your head you may, but be very gentle. As you take energy from the tree, let your own energy flow down your body through your feet to the tree's roots. As new energy flows into your body, old energy will flow out.

Stop when you feel pleasantly charged. Allow any excess to flow down to your feet and out. This exercise usually has a very soothing effect.

Conclusion   Record your observations in your journal.

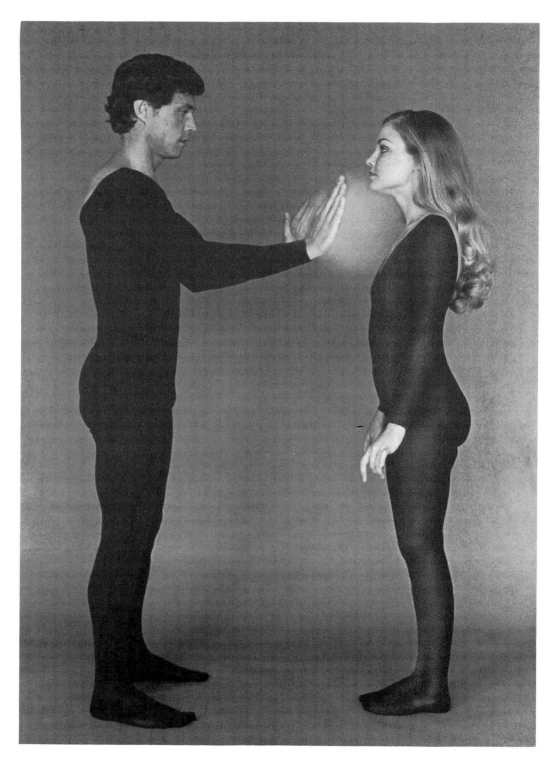

Exercise 9 Increasing a friend's energy.

EXERCISE 9.   FIELD WORK: INCREASING A FRIEND'S ENERGY

Repetitions   Three or more.

Preparation   Read the entire exercise. You and your friend should wear natural-fibre clothing and no jewellery. Stand in the Grounded Position.

Explanation   Now that you know how to transfer energy and how to increase your own energy, you can combine these skills to help other people.

Instructions   Build a globe of energy in the centre of your body. Use your whole energy-body. Focus on the globe. Breathe slowly and evenly. Be sure to generate enough energy, as you do not want to deplete yourself in order to help someone else.

   Now direct the energy up from the centre of your body through both arms and out of your palms. Very gently, with your hands a few inches from your friend, send energy over his entire body, beginning at his feet.

Conclusion   Did you observe any changes in your friend? Did his posture change? Did his eyes get brighter? Record your observations in your journal.

Trouble-shooting   It has happened a few times in our classes that the student has felt tired after being given energy, and this may occur in your case. There are two causes: either the receiver now has too much energy in his body and therefore is getting less energy movement, or the vibration of your energy is not compatible with his. If your friend has too much energy in his body, he may actually feel that his energy has been reduced because the energy flow is stifled. In this case, he simply needs to discharge energy through his feet. Ask him to stand barefoot in the Grounded Position, knees flexed and hips loose. He should vividly see or feel energy slowly flowing down his legs and out of his feet. He should do this gently until he feels better. If the vibrations are not compatible, he should exchange energy with nature. This will cleanse the discordant energy from his body.

Daily Training

Practise Exercise 6: Calisthenics: Flowing Energy Through Your Entire Body, daily. Do not perform the variation until you have practised the exercise for one week.

Exercise 10 Waterfall.

Chapter 2

PSYCHIC CLEANING

You have seen that psychic energy can be transferred from one person to another and can be taken from your environment. Psychic energy can also vibrate to different frequencies and can carry emotions and other information. Perception of the information carried by energy is one of the most important psychic skills. It is basic to any form of psychic activity that involves interaction with other people, such as precognition, healing, and finding people or objects that have been lost. Energy that carries information unrelated to your interest is distracting and interferes with clear psychic perception. We refer to this energy as psychic dirt.

Your energy-body generates energy much as your physical body generates heat. Your energy vibrates at your particular frequency and is as unique as your fingerprint. As you go through the day your thoughts and emotions are reflected through your energy, and psychic energy carrying this information is transferred between people as they communicate. However, after a period of time, excess energy with outdated information on it builds up. This static energy gathers on people's bodies, in rooms, and even on jewellery — particularly gold and silver jewellery. Before doing psychic work, therefore, it is important to remove extraneous energy in order to make perception as clear and easy as possible.

All of us respond to the emotions carried by energy, but because of our different backgrounds, we respond differently. What is positive to one, may be negative to another. Energy, regardless of intent, has to be judged by its effects. Psychic dirt is, in fact, energy that is not good for you. What one person experiences as comforting, sheltering love, another person reacts to as a controlling, smothering emotion. The triggering of anger may explode in wounding hostility, or may open the barrier that has been blocking a person's emotions. We cannot label one emotion as good or bad, or one vibration as clean or dirty. Whether it is positive or negative depends on the person. Nor are good vibrations always compatible. Different people's energies are individual and unique and do not always harmonize. While no one could claim that either green or pink is the better colour, certain shades clash. And so it is with people's energies.

Psychic cleaning can aid in the release of stress. Stress often occurs as a result of difficulty in changing pace. Most of us tend to maintain a behavioural framework beyond the time that it is relevant. Removing old energy, laden with the thoughts and emotions of the working day, makes it easier to leave the work day behind and to relax. Removing the build-up of energy again before work will aid your concentration and focus by reducing the subliminal distractions that energy from old situations can cause.

All of us have had the experience of being negatively affected by another person's emotional outburst. Occasionally a friend needs a shoulder to cry on, or someone to ventilate to. It is easier to provide a willing ear when you know that the effects on you will be minimal because of your ability to remove the negative emotions via psychic cleaning.

Not only does psychic dirt affect you emotionally, it also affects you physically. It can make you feel nervous, tired, or it can cause you to have difficulty in sleeping. As we will show you later in this chapter, it will even cause most people's muscles to weaken in a standard kinesiological test.

Psychic dirt, therefore, can be energy which carries your own emotions reflecting outdated situations or events; it can be energy that carries another person's emotions; it can, in fact, be energy that carries any kind of discordant vibration. This dirt, like static on a radio, interferes with clear psychic perception and can also have physical and emotional effects.

Psychic cleaning is especially important for people in the service professions. Whenever there is a situation in which the client releases energy, physically or emotionally, that energy will gather in the room and on the therapist. A psychically clean room is easy for people to relax in. If you work with many people, psychically cleaning yourself between clients will help you stay more energized and focused. Cleaning yourself at the end of the day will help you to leave your work at the office and not bring those situations and energies home with you.

Patients benefit in many ways also. They will relax more readily in a psychically clean room. They will also be able to focus better and will not be affected by energy from previous clients. Therapists are better able to serve their clients when not distracted by old energies. Benefits to businessmen and teachers apply equally.

EXERCISE 10. SOLO EXERCISE: WATERFALL

Repetitions Do this exercise daily and before any psychic work.

Preparation In this and all subsequent exercises, it will be assumed that you have read the entire exercise and that you are wearing natural-fibre clothing and no jewellery. Stand in the Grounded Position.

Explanation One of the principal methods of causing the energy-body to produce effects is through visualization. Although visualization is important

Exercise 10 Waterfall

and is something that we will be using extensively, please keep in mind that visualization serves to state your goal, and that there is a physical part of you, your energy-body, which will be doing the actual work. Visualization is simply the means by which you tell your energy-body what to do. This meditative visualization serves to direct your energy-body to remove accumulated psychic dirt from your physical body.

Instructions Visualize yourself standing under a waterfall with a river at your feet leading outside. Feel the waterfall wash away all the old emotions and distracting thoughts that have gathered about you during the day. Feel the water splash over your head, shoulders, chest and back, down your legs, and into the stream which then takes the psychic dirt outside. Do this exercise slowly, giving careful attention to each part of your body. After you have completed it once, do it again. When finished, you will have a feeling of lightness and relaxation.

Conclusion Record your observations in your journal.

Variation Some people like to do the Waterfall while they are taking a shower. They find that the water helps clarify their visualization. The dirt is sent down the drain.

EXERCISE 11.   SOLO EXERCISE: SCRAPING

Repetitions   Do this exercise in conjunction with the Waterfall and immediately before doing any psychic work.

Preparation   Have the rock salt ready. Stand in the Grounded Position.

Explanation   Some frequencies of energy are very heavy and require a concentrated effort to remove. You can cleanse this thick crust of psychic dirt from your body by scraping it off with your hands. Use both the Waterfall and Scraping techniques for thorough psychic cleansing. Do the Waterfall first, then follow it with the Scraping technique. The Waterfall cleans loose and newly acquired psychic dirt; Scraping removes heavy, stale psychic dirt. Both techniques are important.

Instructions   Physically scrape along your body, visualizing clearly that your hands are removing the thick layer of old energy. Be aware of the sensation in your palms and fingers as the psychic dirt that you are scraping off builds up on your hands. Toss the dirty energy into a bowl of rock salt as you clean. Keep your hands moving at a ninety degree angle from the surface of your body, so that you are removing the dirt, not rubbing it in. Keep in mind that you are using visualization and the physical scraping motion to focus your energy-body. Your energy-body will remove the psychic dirt. Concentration is important. If you lose focus while you are scraping, then your energy-body will not be able to remove the heavy, static energy. Moving your hands over your body without concentrating will accomplish nothing.

Variation   Many of our students find it helpful to do the Waterfall and Scraping exercises in the shower. In that case, of course, the psychic dirt is directed down the drain.

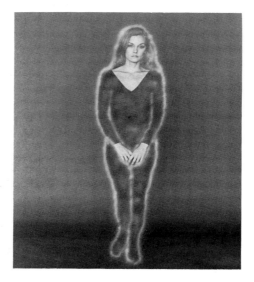

Exercise 11.1   Psychic dirt.

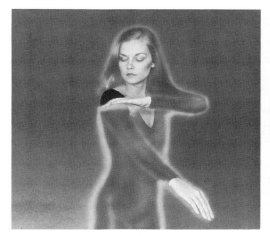

Exercise 11.2   Scraping.

Exercise 11.3   Scraping.

Exercise 11.4   Scraping.

Exercise 11.5   Scraping.

Exercise 11.6   Scraping.

Exercise 11.7   Scraping.

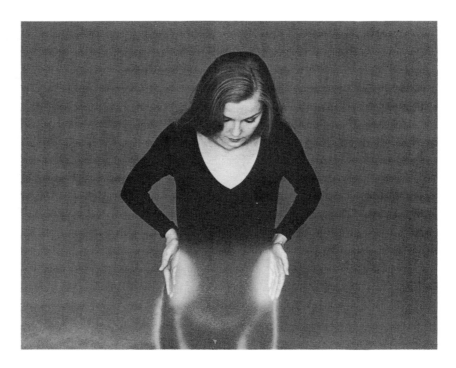

Exercise 11.8 Scraping.

Exercise 11.9 Scraping.

Exercise 11.10 Scraping.

Exercise 11.11 Scraping.

Exercise 11.12 Scraping.

Exercise 11.13 Scraping.

EXERCISE 12. FIELD WORK: PSYCHICALLY CLEANING ANOTHER PERSON

Repetitions   As needed.

Preparation   Have the rock salt ready. Your friend should also wear natural-fibre clothing and remove any jewellery.

Explanation   Now you are ready to use psychic cleansing to help someone else. You will want to do this if the other person is sick, has been through an emotional trauma and is too weak to do the Waterfall and Scraping himself, or has not yet been taught the techniques. To clean another person, use a variation of the Scraping technique.

Cleaner's Instructions   It is important to clean the person in the following order, throwing the dirty energy into the rock salt as you go:

1. Clean both sides of the back, down to the feet. Do not touch the spine.
2. Clean the insides and backs of the legs.
3. Starting at the collar bone, clean the chest and torso.
4. Clean the fronts and sides of the legs.
5. Clean the arms, starting at the shoulders.
6. Clean the spine, starting from the base and going up to the head. Take the energy out from between each vertebra.
7. Scrape the dirty energy upward as you clean the head and neck.

When you have finished, your friend will feel lighter and more relaxed. Be sure to psychically clean yourself afterwards.

Conclusion   Get feedback from your friend. Record your observations in your journal.

Trouble-shooting   When you are cleansing another person, be careful not to absorb any psychic dirt. You may even want to imagine that you are wearing rubber gloves.

Variation   When people are sick, negative energy builds up around them. Their own bad feelings and other people's worries create psychic dirt on their bodies. Removing the negative energy will make the sick person feel better. When cleaning a sick person, you must be particularly gentle. It may not be possible to clean the sick person's whole body at once. He may be too weak. In this case, several partial cleanings are indicated.

If you do not have rock salt – perhaps in a hospital room – turn on the water tap and run the psychic dirt down the sink, or visualize a great wind blowing the dirt out of the window (Exercise 13).

The sick person should be cleaned three or four times a day if this can be managed. Aches and other unpleasant symptoms will be relieved, and he will sleep better.

It is very important to clean yourself after working with a sick person. Be sure to do the Waterfall and Scraping techniques thoroughly.

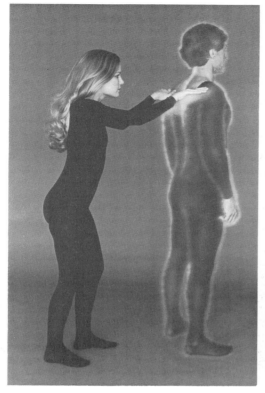

Exercise 12.1 Cleaning another person.

Exercise 12.2 Cleaning another person.

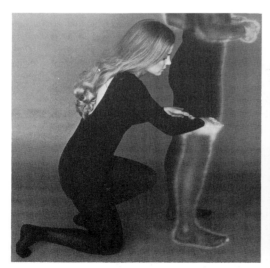

Exercise 12.3 Cleaning another person.

Exercise 12.4 Cleaning another person.

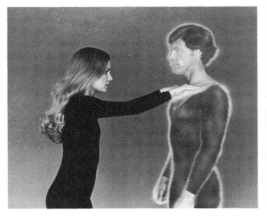

Exercise 12.5 Cleaning another person.

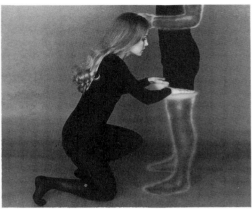

Exercise 12.6 Cleaning another person.

Exercise 12.7 Cleaning another person.

Exercise 12.8 Cleaning another person.

Exercise 12.9 Cleaning another person.

Exercise 12.10 Cleaning another person.

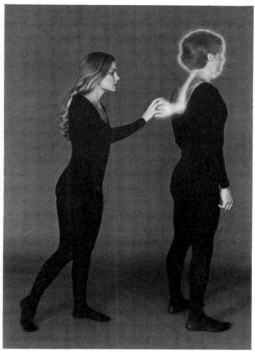

Exercise 12.11 Cleaning another person.

Exercise 12.12 Cleaning another person.

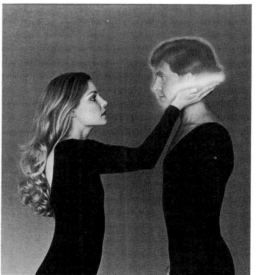

Exercise 12.13 Cleaning another person.

Exercise 12.14   Cleaning another person.

EXERCISE 13.   PSYCHICALLY CLEANING A ROOM

Repetitions   As needed.

Preparation   Open the doors and windows. Stand in the Grounded Position in the centre of the room.

Explanation   Just as static energy accumulates on your body, it will accumulate in your room. As you go through your normal activities, the energy that you generate, carrying your thoughts and feelings, gathers in your environment. Rooms where groups of people meet collect many kinds of energy. It is important to keep your environment psychically clean.

Cleaner's Instructions, Wind Visualization   You will focus your energy-body and use your energy to move a physical substance – psychic dirt. To do this, vividly visualize a great wind sweeping past you, blowing old energy out of the door. Feel the force of this tremendous gale as it moves past you. It is blowing through the entire room from floor to ceiling, taking all the dirty energy and pushing it outside. Be aware of the sound of this great wind. Because of its force, the wind moves psychic dirt out of all of the furniture – curtains, rugs, lampshades – and from places you cannot even see – behind and under the

 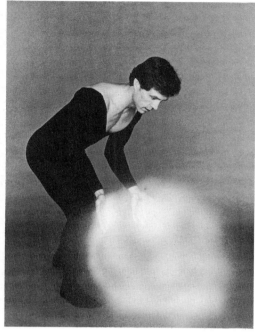

Exercise 13.1 Wind visualization.   *Exercise 13.2* Cleaning a room — scraping.

couch, the bookcases, the cupboards. Be aware of the cool, clean wind blowing throughout the room. Smell the crisp, fresh air entering the room.

Repeat. You will find that the exercise becomes easier as more old dirt is moved out.

Cleaner's Instructions, Scraping Just as you need to scrape heavy energy off your body, you will need to scrape the heavy energy out of your room. Find the places where people sit most often. Those will be the places that have the most static energy. Begin in the Grounded Position. Move through the room, scraping the energy before you and out of the door.

Does your room feel brighter? More spacious? Fresher? You will find that life is pleasanter and psychic work is easier in a clean environment.

Conclusion Clean (Waterfall and Scraping). Record your observations in your journal.

EXERCISE 14. PSYCHIC CLEANING OF JEWELLERY

Repetitions   Six or more.

Preparation   Have the rock salt ready. Clean (Waterfall and Scraping). Sit in the Grounded Position opposite your partner.

Explanation   Just as energy gathers on bodies and in rooms, it gathers on objects such as jewellery. Gold and silver, in particular, gather quantities of energy. Because energy on jewellery carries the vibration of any emotion we have felt while wearing it, and because we are all influenced by energy vibrations, dirty jewellery affects us physically and emotionally. It can make a person feel tired, or nervous, or uncomfortable. Cleaning jewellery is, therefore, an important psychic skill, contributing to your health and comfort and serving as a first step towards learning psychometry.

Perceiver's Instructions   Hold a ring or bracelet loosely in your hand and sense the energy that is on it. You may wish to close your eyes for better concentration. Be open to any images that arise. These images are your response to the energy. Relax and trust yourself. Information will come. Does the jewellery feel hot? Heavy? Rough? Prickly? Write down your perceptions and hand the jewellery to your partner. Clean your hands.

Cleaner's Instructions   Get a sense of the energy on the jewellery. Note down your perceptions; then build up energy. Hold the jewellery loosely in the fingers of one hand over a bowl of rock salt. Direct a beam of energy from the index finger of your other hand on to the jewellery. Use this beam to push off the old static energy in the same way that you use the Waterfall to clean your body. Now scrape the excess energy off the jewellery and toss it into the bowl. If the jewellery is extremely dirty you may have to pull off the loosened dirt several times. Remember that a clean piece of jewellery is one that has no energy on it at all. Note down any differences in your perception of the jewellery. Hand it to the Perceiver.

Perceiver's Instructions   Hold the article of jewellery lightly in your hand again. Be aware of its weight and its temperature. Is it lighter? Calmer? Cooler? Smoother? Write down your perceptions.

Conclusion   Compare notes. Change roles and repeat, using a different article of jewellery. Synthesize and record your observations in your journal.

Trouble-shooting   Perhaps you were not confident of your perceptions in this exercise. Such a feeling is normal. Any new skill must be tried and tested before we feel comfortable in relying on it. Trust is built through experience. We commonly check our physical perceptions both with other people and with our physical senses. If you hear a sound, you go and look to see what has caused it. In the same way, you need to check your new psychic perceptions. The next exercise provides a method for checking your perception of clean and dirty jewellery.

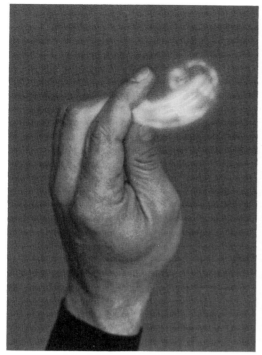

Exercise 14.1 Psychic dirt on jewellery.

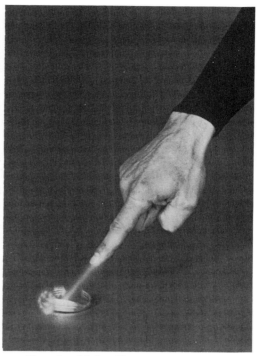

Exercise 14.2 Cleaning jewellery.

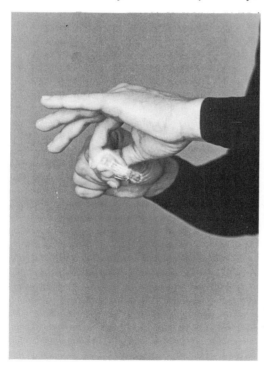

Exercise 14.3 Cleaning jewellery.

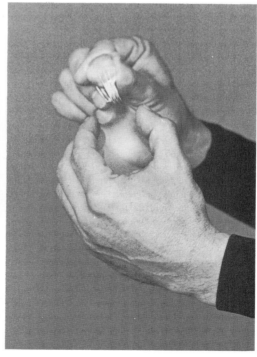

Exercise 14.4 Cleaning jewellery.

EXERCISE 15. MUSCLE TEST

Repetitions Six or more.

Preparation Have the rock salt ready. Clean (Waterfall and Scraping). Have psychically dirty jewellery at hand.

Explanation For this exercise it is best to use plain gold or silver jewellery that has been worn over a long period of time. Jewellery that has a quantity of energy on it can cause muscular weakness. The weakening effect of psychically dirty jewellery is easily demonstrated by a standard muscle test. The object of this test is to isolate one muscle and test its relative strength both with and without the presence of psychically dirty jewellery; the point of the exercise is to illustrate that psychic dirt can have a weakening effect on your body.

Responder's Instructions Stand with your arm out from your body at a ninety degree angle. Keep your arm straight in front and level, with your fingers extended. Do not let your arm move. If it goes too far to the side or too far up, or if you clench your fist, different muscles will be brought into play and the test will not be accurate. The comparative strength or weakness of your arm will show whether or not the energy is bad for you. Keep in mind that this is not a test of physical strength; it is, rather, an easy way to judge the effect of psychic dirt. Be methodical and objective, and note down the results as you go along.

Cleaner's Instructions Ask the Responder to resist as you push down on his arm gently but firmly, using a gradual pressure and a gradual release. Do you

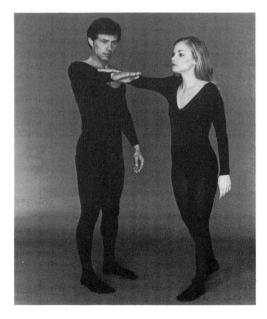

Exercise 15 Muscle test.

have a sense of how strong this muscle is? When you know what his basic strength is, it is possible to gauge the effect of psychic dirt. Now give him an article of psychically dirty jewellery to wear on the arm that you are testing. Use the same gradual pressure you used earlier. Push down on the arm again as he resists. If the energy on the jewellery is not good for him, it will be harder for him to resist the same amount of pressure. Be careful not to let your opinion of whether he should be weak or strong influence the amount of pressure you use. Be methodical and objective and note down your results.

Now ask him to remove the jewellery. Clean it over the bowl of salt, and test him again. Is he stronger than when the jewellery was dirty? Be careful to use the same amount of pressure throughout the test.

Conclusion Change roles and repeat the test, using various articles of jewellery. Synthesize and record your observations in your journal.

Trouble-shooting Some of the uncleaned jewellery will probably not have a weakening effect on the Responder. This means that for the Responder, the energy on that article of jewellery is not dirty energy. Different energy-bodies respond differently to various kinds of energy.

Advanced Variation: Physical Effects of Emotions on Energy
Repeat the above exercise using jewellery that is psychically clean. You will want to do the muscle test to be sure that the jewellery is clean. Then you will generate emotion-laden energy and direct it on to the jewellery. (See Exercise 17. Perceiving Emotions on Jewellery. You may wish to defer practising this variation until you have completed Exercise 17.)

Select an emotion that you can recreate in yourself easily. You may want to relive an event mentally. As you experience this emotion, direct energy up from the centre of your body, down your arm, and out of your finger on to the article of jewellery you are holding. Your energy carries the emotion on to the gold or silver jewellery where it will remain until you clean it. Be sure to give no clue as to what the emotion is. Now ask your partner to put on the article of jewellery; then test the strength of his muscle as before. You will want to play with this exercise, using many different emotions. Probably you will find that you do not always get the results you might logically expect. Some apparently positive emotions may cause your partner to weaken; some apparently negative ones may have no effect. One of the disconcerting results of this experiment is that it shows that in using psychic energy, as in doing anything else, good intentions alone are not enough. Jewellery that has too much energy on it, regardless of the emotion, may be weakening in itself. You may even wish to try the results with jewellery that has a great deal of energy on it, but no emotion at all.

Daily Training
Practise Exercises 10: Waterfall and 11: Scraping.
After cleaning, practise Exercise 6: Calisthenics: Flowing Energy Through Your Entire Body.

Exercise 17 Psychometry — perceiving emotions on jewellery.

Chapter 3

PSYCHIC COMMUNICATION

You have seen that different vibrations and emotions are carried by psychic energy. As you practise the exercises in this chapter, you will learn to transmit information consciously by energy that you send to another person. This technique is useful in situations when you wish to make your presence or attitude felt without saying a word. Teachers and entertainers are frequently noted for having this kind of skill. You will also learn to perceive and interpret the information that people transmit by their energy. This kind of perception is for many people almost the definition of being psychic. Indeed, communication is of paramount importance. However, many people misunderstand what psychic communication and perception are. Very often people expect a psychic to read their minds and to relate the thoughts that are found there. The human mind is rich and varied and is ever moving. Very seldom is a person's mental focus strong enough or of long enough duration for the reading of thoughts to be practical, since such reading requires a very strong and highly focused sender. Most people's thoughts are guided by and mingled with their emotions which are generally stronger and of longer duration than their thoughts. Therefore, reading emotions is both easier to learn and more practical to use than reading thoughts. You will find it easier to perceive someone's hidden fear or pleasure than to perceive his ideas about the economy or foreign policy. Keep in mind that psychic skills are performed by the non-linear part of the brain, which is creative, not logical.

By practising the exercises in this chapter, you will increase your general responsiveness to other people's feelings. You will be able to experience another person's emotions in a very direct and immediate way. You will also learn to direct your empathy so that your sensitivity is an asset, not a burden. As you work with these exercises, keep in mind that psychic perception comes to people in many different ways. Usually, our bodies provide a sensory translation of psychic information. You may receive an image, a kinaesthetic feeling, or a sound. Whatever you perceive will be your body's attempt to show you the information that is carried by the energy. It is necessary to experiment and discover your own individual mode of psychic perception and develop it until it becomes thoroughly reliable. It is important that you work from your strengths. If you are tone deaf, do not expect sound to be your area of psychic perception. If you are colour-blind, do not expect colour to be part of your psychic vocabulary. Only those people who excel at visual symbology may look profitably for visions. Certainly it is necessary to improve our weak areas, but excellence is achieved in our areas of strength.

EXERCISE 16. CALISTHENICS: FLOWER TO BUD

Repetitions   Do this exercise before doing any psychic work.

Preparation   Clean (Waterfall and Scraping).

Explanation   The object of this exercise is to help you focus your energy-body so that psychic perception and strength will come more easily to you. To be psychologically open does not mean that you should have an open, loose energy-body. In order to be effective, the energy-body must be focused. This exercise will tone your energy-body and give you control.

Instructions   Vividly visualize that you are a many-petalled flower in its fullest bloom. Then curl the petals gently back to the centre, one by one, as the flower gradually becomes a bud again.

Conclusion   Record your observations in your journal.

Trouble-shooting   Occasionally students feel tense and constricted after doing this exercise. Sometimes, also, a student has a headache. This indicates that the bud has been closed too tightly. If this happens to you, you should repeat the visualization and open the bud slightly. If you frequently experience these symptoms, it indicates that your energy-body is congested. You should regularly perform Exercise 6: Flowing Energy Through Your Entire Body.

EXERCISE 17. PERCEIVING EMOTIONS ON JEWELLERY (PSYCHOMETRY)

Preparation   Have the rock salt ready. Clean (Waterfall and Scraping). Flower to Bud. Sit opposite your partner in the Grounded Position. You will need a small article of gold or silver jewellery which has been psychically cleaned.

Explanation   In this exercise you will learn to transmit emotionally charged energy on to jewellery, using a variety of emotions. You will also learn to read the emotions that have been put on the jewellery. This exercise will increase your ability to transmit clearly and will develop both your control and your perception of energy. During the first few sendings, the Perceiver will discover in what ways his psychic perception works; subsequently, he will distinguish between positive and negative emotions; and, finally, he will describe his responses to the Sender and specify the emotion sent.

Exercise 17 Psychometry — perceiving emotions on jewellery.

Part One: Sensing Emotions

Repetitions Four or more.

Sender's Instructions Select an emotion that you can vividly recreate in yourself. Be sure the emotion you choose is a strong and simple one such as love or hate, fear or happiness. You and your partner are just learning; this is not the time for subtleties. Experience the emotion. You may want to remember an event associated with it. As you are experiencing the emotion, allow your energy to flow down your arm on to the jewellery you are holding. As you know, energy carries emotion and your feeling is thus transmitted on to the jewellery. Hand the jewellery to your partner. Clean your hands between sendings. When your partner has a clear sense of the energy on the jewellery, describe to him the emotion you put on it.

Perceiver's Instructions Hold the article of jewellery loosely in your hand and make yourself as receptive as possible. Close your eyes and breathe deeply and regularly. Whatever you perceive will be your body's attempt to show you the information that is carried on the jewellery. When you have a clear sense of the energy, ask your partner what emotion he put on it so that you can begin to identify and translate your psychic perceptions. It is very important that you clean your hands and the jewellery between sendings so that the new information does not have to filter through the old.

Conclusion When both of you have clearly established how another person's basic emotions feel to you psychically, record your observations in your journal and move on to Part Two.

Trouble-shooting Everyone responds to the emotions carried by energy. The challenge is in allowing yourself to be open to the information; the skill is in learning to interpret that information. Your psychic perception is in an early stage of development, as is your ability to interpret. It will take practice for you to understand the signals your body sends you.

Variation An alternate method of reading emotions on jewellery is to place the article on the centre of your forehead instead of in your hand (see Appendix for a cautionary note about using the head).

Part Two: Distinguishing Between Positive and Negative Emotions
Repetitions Six or more.

Sender's Instructions Put a clear strong emotion on the jewellery. It is a good idea to use an emotion you have shown the Perceiver before. You must be careful to give no clue either by facial expression or body language as to what the emotion is.

Perceiver's Instructions Perceive whether the emotion is positive or negative and tell the Sender your perceptions.

Conclusion Change roles and repeat. Record your observations in your journal. When you feel confident of your ability to perceive categories of emotion, move on to Part Three.

Part Three: Distinguishing Specific Emotions
Repetitions Six or more.

Sender's Instructions Select an emotion. Experience it as you generate and direct energy on to the jewellery. Take care to give no clue as to what the emotion is.

Perceiver's Instructions Describe your psychic perception and specify the emotion on the jewellery. Be careful to clean your hands and the jewellery between sendings.

Conclusion Change roles and repeat. Record your observations in your journal.

Variation You will enjoy testing your perceptual ability. Blindfold the Perceiver so that body language or eye contact can offer no possible clue. You may even want to have the Sender charge the jewellery while the Perceiver is in another room, and then have the Perceiver read the emotion while the Sender is in the other room.

EXERCISE 18.   DIRECT ENERGY PERCEPTION

Repetitions   Six or more.

Preparation   Have the rock salt ready. Clean (Waterfall and Scraping). Flower to Bud. Sit in the Grounded Position opposite your partner.

Explanation   Now you will send and perceive emotion-charged energy without the aid of jewellery.

Sender's Instructions   Select a clear strong emotion and then develop that emotion in yourself. Let the emotion-charged energy flow down your right arm and direct the energy with your forefinger into the Perceiver's hand (Exercise 1). Be careful to give no clue as to what the emotion is. Clean your hands between sendings, and alternate hands.

Perceiver's Instructions   Hold your hand out to receive your partner's energy. Relax and focus on your perception. How readily can you distinguish between positive and negative emotions? How well are you able to specify the emotion? Remember to clean your hands between each sending and to alternate hands.

Conclusion   Change roles and repeat. Record your observations in your journal.

EXERCISE 19.   EMOTIONS AND PHYSICAL STRENGTH

Repetitions   Six or more.

Preparation   Clean (Waterfall and Scraping). Flower to Bud. Stand in the Grounded Position.

Explanation   The emotions that people send to us by energy can even affect the physical strength of our bodies, whether we are consciously aware of the nature of the emotion being sent or not. We influence each other profoundly in this subtle way. In this exercise, you will deliberately send emotions and use the muscle test to discern their effects on physical strength.

Sender's Instructions   Make a list of emotions you plan to generate. It is easier if these are emotions you have sent before. As always, the emotions you choose should be clear, strong, and easily distinguishable. In this exercise you should personalize the emotions as much as possible, directing them specifically to your partner. It is essential that you give no body language clues and that you monitor yourself as you are doing the muscle test in order to use the same amount of pressure every time.

Generate the emotion, and when you feel it clearly, visualize the emotion-laden energy emanating from your whole body like a fog, surrounding your partner entirely.

Now perform the muscle test.

Generate and test several times. As with the jewellery test, you may have unexpected results.

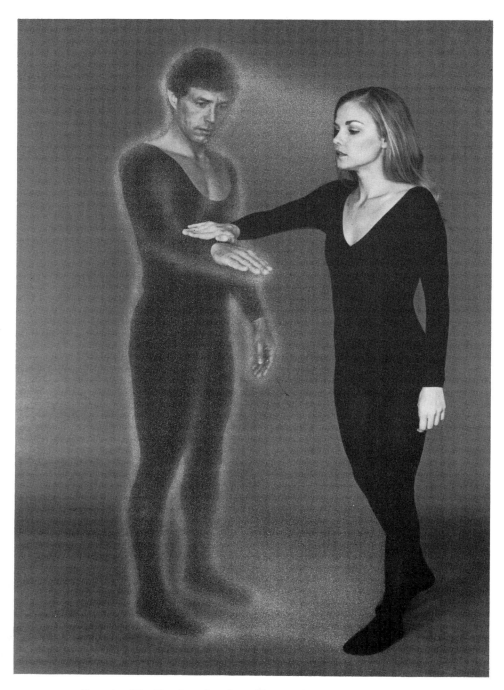

Exercise 19 Testing for the effects of emotion on energy.

Responder's Instructions Remember to hold the arm that is being tested at a right angle, as before. If your arm goes too far to the side or too far up, or if you clench your fist, different muscles will be brought into play and the test will not be accurate. Be sure to resist with the same amount of pressure each time you are tested and to change arms if you become tired. Keep in mind that this is a test of the effects of emotion-laden energy on the body; it is not a test of your or your partner's strength. It is not necessary to read the emotion on the energy your partner sends to you; merely allow yourself to respond.

Conclusion Clean. Change roles and repeat. Record your observations in your journal.

EXERCISE 20. PERCEIVING MUSICAL TONES ON ENERGY

Preparation Have the rock salt ready. Clean (Waterfall and Scraping). Flower to Bud. Sit opposite your partner in the Grounded Position. You may want to listen to a few scales before you begin this exercise.

Explanation Now you know that psychic energy can transmit emotions. It can also transmit information that is more intellectual and even more specific. Because energy can vibrate at different frequencies it is easy to use it to communicate musical sounds. Musical sounds are ideal data to transmit because a wide range of musical tones can be sent and read exactly. During the first few sendings the Perceiver will be establishing a base line and discovering how energy frequency is translated into musical sound; subsequently, he will distinguish between high tones and low tones; and finally, he will specify the tone and hum it out loud.

Part One: Sensing Musical Tones
Repetitions Four or more.

Sender's Instructions Mentally sound a tone. Draw energy, with the tone on it, through your arm and out of your finger into your partner's hand. Hear the tone clearly in your mind as you send the energy. This will cause the energy to vibrate at that frequency. When the Perceiver has a clear sense of the energy, hum the note aloud. Alternate between high and low notes. Clean your hands after each sending.

Perceiver's Instructions Hold your hand relaxed and open on your knee. Allow yourself to be open to perceptions. When you have a clear sense of the energy, let your partner know. He will then hum the note. This will help you learn how to translate the vibration into sound. You may find that the high tones feel sharp and piercing while the lower tones feel wider and pulsing. Be sure to clean your hands after each sending.

Conclusion Change roles and repeat. When both of you have clearly established how you perceive musical tones sent by energy, record your observations and move on to Part Two.

Part Two: Distinguishing Between High and Low Tones

Repetitions   Six or more.

Instructions   The Sender transmits a silent scale by energy. The Perceiver discerns whether the scale is moving up or down. Then, after adequate practice, the Sender transmits a single tone and the Perceiver discerns whether it is high or low. As always, watch your body language. Do not forget to clean between transmissions and to alternate hands.

Conclusion   Change roles and repeat. Record your observations in your journal and move on to Part Three.

Part Three: Distinguishing Specific Notes

Repetitions   Six or more.

Instructions   The Sender directs a clear, silent energy tone. The Perceiver distinguishes the tone precisely and hums it out loud. Again, watch your body language; remember to alternate hands; and clean between sendings.

Conclusion   Change roles and repeat. Record your observations in your journal.

Trouble-shooting   It may happen in the beginning that the Sender projects a tone, for example middle C, and the Perceiver consistently reads it an octave higher or lower than it is. This sometimes occurs because people send and receive more readily within their own vocal range. A Perceiver with a soprano vocal range may unconsciously translate a low tone to a higher octave. Familiarity with your partner's vibration and practice with the technique will solve this problem if it arises.

Advanced Variation   The Sender silently transmits melodies, beginning with something simple, such as 'London Bridge', and later progressing to something more complex. The Perceiver hums the melodies.

EXERCISE 21   PERCEIVING COLOUR ON ENERGY

Preparation   Have the rock salt ready. Clean (Waterfall and Scraping). Flower to Bud. Sit opposite your partner in the Grounded Position.

Explanation   Another method of developing keen energy perception is to work with colour carried by energy. In this exercise you will use the spectrum instead of the scale.

Part One: Sensing Colour

Repetitions   Four or more.

Sender's Instructions   Use clear, contrasting colours: red and blue, green and orange, violet and yellow. Direct the energy, clearly visualizing a colour.

When the Perceiver has a sense of the energy vibration, identify the colour. Clean your hands after each sending.

Perceiver's Instructions Be sure your hands are relaxed. Allow yourself to be responsive to the energy. You may wish to close your eyes. When you have a clear sense of the energy, tell your partner. He will identify the colour he has transmitted to help you establish a base line. Clean your hands after each sending.

Conclusion Change roles and repeat. When both of you have clearly established how you perceive colour sent by energy, record your observations and move on to Part Two.

Part Two: Distinguishing Specific Colours
Repetitions Six or more.

Instructions Perceiver specifies the colour that the Sender has transmitted.

Conclusion Change roles and repeat. Record your observations in your journal.

Daily Training
Practise the following exercises daily, in this sequence:
Exercise 10. Waterfall
Exercise 11. Scraping
Exercise 16. Calisthenics: Flower to Bud
Exercise 6. Calisthenics: Flowing Energy Through Your Entire Body, Variation

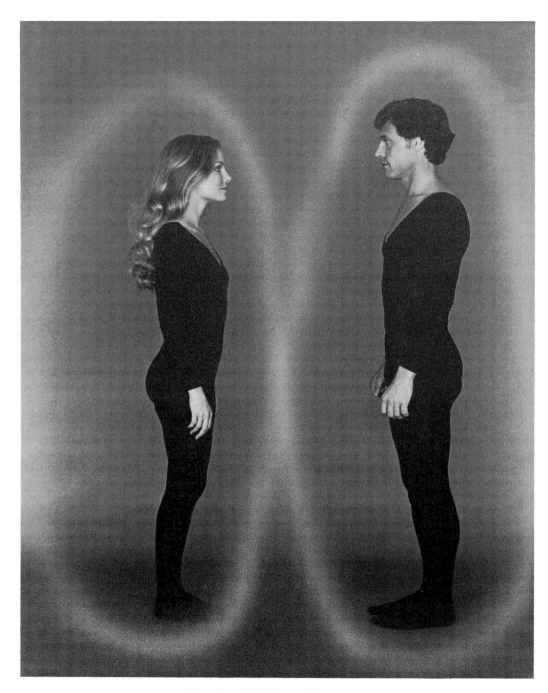

Exercise 25 Energy Rapport.

Chapter 4

PSYCHIC TUNING

You have learned how to perceive and interpret information that is transmitted by energy. In this chapter you will learn how to harmonize your own energy, how to perfect your techniques for increasing a friend's energy, how to set up sympathetic energy flows with other people, how to affect another person's emotional state with psychic energy, and how to harmonize a group.

Each person's energy is composed of a range of frequencies which makes up a particular vibration that is unique to that individual. Because we exchange energy in every human contact, there is always a certain amount of energy in our bodies that has not been converted to our own vibration. Tuning to yourself converts all the energy in your body to your own natural vibration. Tuning energy to another person allows you to give him energy which does not have to be converted to his own vibration and can thus be used immediately.

Energy rapport is essential for empathy. It allows you to mingle another person's energy with your own in order to facilitate communication with him. It allows you to mingle the energies of all the people in a group in order to facilitate group communication. It also enables you to control a potentially negative or even hostile atmosphere. The techniques in this chapter are especially useful to people who work with the public.

EXERCISE 22. SOLO EXERCISE: TUNING TO YOURSELF

Repetitions As needed.

Preparation Clean (Waterfall and Scraping). Flower to Bud. Sit in the Grounded Position.

Explanation It is normal in our daily interaction to exchange energy with the environment around us and with other people. Each person's energy is composed of many different vibrations. As you exchange energy with other people, you absorb many foreign vibrations. Although your body will eventually homogenize and smooth out these foreign vibrations, tuning to yourself speeds the process and is like an internal psychic cleaning. It is a particularly important exercise for those who interact with many people every day and for those who tend to be much influenced or affected by other people's energies. You will find that keeping well tuned makes you feel stronger, more at harmony with yourself, and calmer. If you are under the weather, do not forget to tune to yourself. Oddly enough, it is often difficult to feel your own vibration even though it is what your body knows best. To tune to yourself, you must harmonize your energy and return all parts of yourself to your own individual vibration. This is most easily done by choosing a symbolic image. Since you have used symbolic images in your earlier psychic work, you should know what kinds of images are most comfortable for you.

Instructions Touch your energy-body gently to get a sense of your own vibration. Choose an image to represent it. You may wish to use a colour, a tone, or a tactile sensation. If you have chosen to visualize yourself as a colour, see yourself as gradually becoming that colour all through your body. Begin at your toes and slowly progress up your body, returning each part of yourself to your chosen colour. Take your time. If you have chosen to visualize yourself as a tone, you will want to hear that tone throughout your body, beginning with your feet. Be aware that any other tones in your body will gradually change frequencies until your entire body vibrates only to your chosen note. When all the frequencies in your body have been resolved to your own vibration, you are tuned.

Conclusion Are you aware of any changes in the way you feel? Record your observations in your journal.

EXERCISE 23. TUNING ENERGY TO ANOTHER PERSON

Repetitions Six or more.

Preparation Have the rock salt ready. Clean (Waterfall and Scraping). Flower to Bud. Sit opposite your partner in the Grounded Position.

Explanation In Exercises 20 and 21 you learned to distinguish between different tones and between different colours transmitted by energy. In Exercise 22 you learned to harmonize your own energy – to tune to yourself. Now you will learn to alter your natural vibration in order to harmonize energy with another person. There may be a time when you wish to help someone by giving him energy. Energy that is tuned to his personal vibration is readily absorbed, creates no strain on his energy-body, and is immediately usable. If you give energy to a sick person, it is imperative that you tune it exactly.

Tuner's Instructions First it is necessary to get a sense of your partner's energy. Put your hand near his body and feel his vibration. You may even wish to take energy from your partner as you did in Exercise 2. Be aware of the many different vibrations and variations that make up his personal energy tone. Take your time. You may wish to clean your hands and check his

Exercise 23.1   Sensing your partner's energy.

Exercise 23.2   Tuning energy to another person.

Exercise 23.3   Giving tuned energy.

Exercise 23.4   Absorbing tuned energy.

vibration several times until you are familiar with the tones or colours of your partner's energy.

When you have perceived your partner's energy clearly, generate energy between your hands and tune that energy to his vibration, just as you tuned to colour and sound. When the energy between your hands is vibrating to your partner's frequency, give the energy to him.

Perceiver's Instructions Perceive the energy that the Tuner has given you. When he has succeeded in tuning well, the sensation will be very subtle. It will feel like your own energy in motion. The perception of transmitted energy which you have experienced in Exercises 1 and 2 was, in part, a reading of a foreign vibration entering your body. When you feel that the energy is tuned to you, absorb it into your hand. If the energy feels harsh, or if you feel any discomfort such as a stiffness in your joints, then the Tuner needs more practice.

Conclusion Change roles and repeat. Record your observations in your journal.

Trouble-shooting Occasionally a student will absorb too much discordant energy. If this happens to you, you may ache or feel restless or irritable. In that case, you will want to exchange energy with nature (Exercise 8).

Variation Repeat Exercise 9: Increasing a Friend's Energy. This time, tune the energy to him. Do you observe any differences in the effectiveness of the exercise? Record your observations in your journal.

EXERCISE 24. EXPERIMENT WITH TUNED AND UNTUNED ENERGY

Repetitions One or two.

Preparation Clean (Waterfall and Scraping). Flower to Bud. Tune to yourself. Stand in the Grounded Position.

Explanation The purpose of this exercise is to illustrate the different effects of absorbing large quantities of untuned energy and of absorbing large quantities of tuned energy.

Part One: Absorbing Untuned Energy
Sender's Instructions Build up energy in the centre of your body. Visualize your energy as being clearly distinct from your partner's and direct it out through your palms, gently sending it over your partner's entire body.

Perceiver's Instructions Absorb the energy that your partner gives you and pay close attention to the way that you feel. Monitor your responses for five or ten minutes. Then tune to yourself.

Conclusion Record your observations in your journal. Without changing roles move directly to Part Two of this exercise.

Part Two: Absorbing Tuned Energy

Preparation   Tune to yourself, then Clean (Waterfall and Scraping).

Sender's Instructions   Sense your partner's energy as you did in Exercise 23. Be aware of the different frequencies that make up his personal energy. You may wish to visualize these frequencies as colours or tones. You may wish your partner to give you energy in order to make your perception more distinct. When you have a clear sense of his personal vibration, give him energy that you have tuned to that vibration, sending it gently over his whole body.

Perceiver's Instructions   Absorb the energy that your partner gives you. Carefully observe how you feel. Compare your sensations with those you had when you absorbed untuned energy.

Conclusion   Change roles and repeat the entire experiment. Record your observations in your journal.

EXERCISE 25. FIELD WORK: ENERGY RAPPORT (FIGURE EIGHT METHOD)

Repetitions   Six or more.

Preparation   Clean (Waterfall and Scraping). Flower to Bud. Stand in the Grounded Position.

Explanation   In Exercise 23, you learned to tune to another person. This was done in a controlled situation, in a clean environment, and with a knowledgeable partner. A certain amount of harmonizing of energies can also be achieved even in a dirty environment and with an unknowing participant.

When doing Field Work, it is often impossible to perform the complete Preparation. It may be that you will even have to do Field Work while wearing synthetic-fibre clothing. Psychic work is more difficult to perform under these circumstances and is fatiguing, but is possible. While Cleaning and Flower to Bud enhance your psychic capacity, you may omit them when necessary and simply use the Grounded Position. Since your energy-body is under greater stress when you do not perform the complete Preparation, the Grounded Position is particularly important. Using it will reduce the stress on your energy-body.

Energy Rapport is achieved by setting up an energy flow with another person that is a combination of his energy and your own. This mingling of energies generally eases communication. The exercise may be done whenever you want to set up a sympathetic energy flow with another person; lessen defensiveness, either his or your own; or, in general, facilitate communication. Figure Eight tuning harmonizes energies while leaving each individual's space intact.

Instructions   Visualize energy moving below your friend's feet, up his back, down in front of his body at an angle, beneath your feet, and up your back. The two of you are in a circulating pattern of energy. Once you get the energy flowing, little effort will be needed to keep it moving. You will notice a marked improvement in your communication with the other person because the energy that is being given off from his body is now mingling with your own energy. This causes a general harmonizing effect akin to tuning.

Trouble-shooting If the other person becomes lightheaded or sleepy, you are probably using too much force and energy.

Occasionally a person will unconsciously resist the harmonizing of energies. In such cases it is generally wisest not to try to force the Rapport. However, Energy Rapport is not dangerous, and if you make a mistake and try to tune to a resisting person, the worst that can happen is that he will feel uncomfortable. For your own comfort, we suggest that you do not use Energy Rapport with a person who is excessively dirty, sick, or depressed. Should you set up a sympathetic energy flow with such a person, he will probably feel better; you will probably feel worse. You will then need to clean, take energy from nature, and tune to yourself.

Advanced Variation Transmit emotion-laden energy in the Figure Eight pattern. See in what way the other person's mood is affected as you transmit calmness, comradery, or excitement by the energy. You may find that you can soothe an angry person, calm a nervous one, or stimulate a bored one.

EXERCISE 26. FIELD WORK: ENERGY RAPPORT (CIRCLE METHOD)

Repetitions Three or more.

Preparation Clean (Waterfall and Scraping). Flower to Bud. Stand in the Grounded Position.

Explanation When tuning to a person with whom you have close ties, you will find the Circle Method effective. The Figure Eight Method may be used even with strangers. They will not feel threatened because the flow of energy from body to body in the Figure Eight Method is somewhat indirect and leaves space between two people. The Circle Method, however, causes the flow of energy to move more directly from body to body and harmonizes the energies more completely. It is, therefore, very effective for people who are used to your energy and with whom you are intimate, but it may seem intrusive to others.

Instructions Create a band of energy about twelve inches wide, which moves in a clockwise direction at waist level, encircling you and your friend. Once the energy is moving it will continue for some time with only minimal attention.

Conclusion Record your observations in your journal.

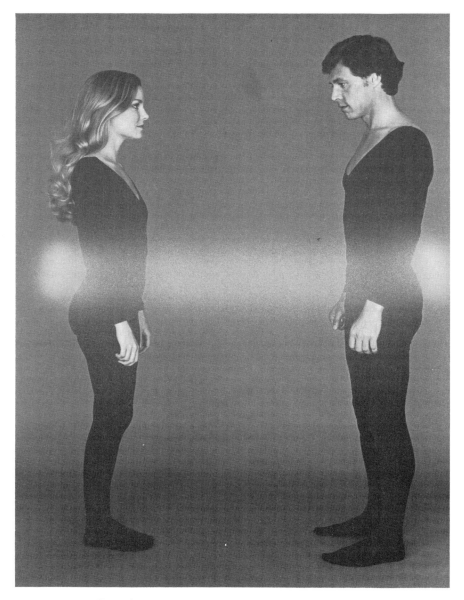

Exercise 26   Energy rapport — circle method.

Energy Rapport Variations

Advanced Variation A   You will want to experiment with Energy Rapport techniques. Try using both the Figure Eight and Circle Methods with strangers and with friends. Observe the different effects.

Advanced Variation B   As you work with Energy Rapport techniques, you will also want to develop your perception by reading the emotions you find on the energy. Check your perception as much as possible.

EXERCISE 27. FIELD WORK: ENERGY RAPPORT (HARMONIZING A GROUP)

Repetitions Three or more.

Preparation Clean (Waterfall and Scraping). Flower to Bud. Stand or sit in the Grounded Position.

Explanation This exercise is useful for facilitating communication within a group. As you have seen, it is not difficult to set energy in motion. One person alone can harmonize a group in this way. You may wish to use this exercise often in your ordinary interactions. Because the whole group is being tuned together, no one is likely to feel that his individual space is being encroached upon.

Instructions Visualize a wind sweeping clockwise from behind your body, through and around the group. The wind will blend and harmonize the different vibrations. When the energy is moving freely, only occasional attention will be necessary to keep the flow in motion.

Conclusion Record your observations in your journal.

Daily Training
Practise the following exercises daily, in this sequence:
Exercises 10: Waterfall and 11: Scraping
Exercise 16: Calisthenics: Flower to Bud
Exercise 22: Tuning to Yourself
Exercise 6: Calisthenics: Flowing Energy Through Your Entire Body, Variation

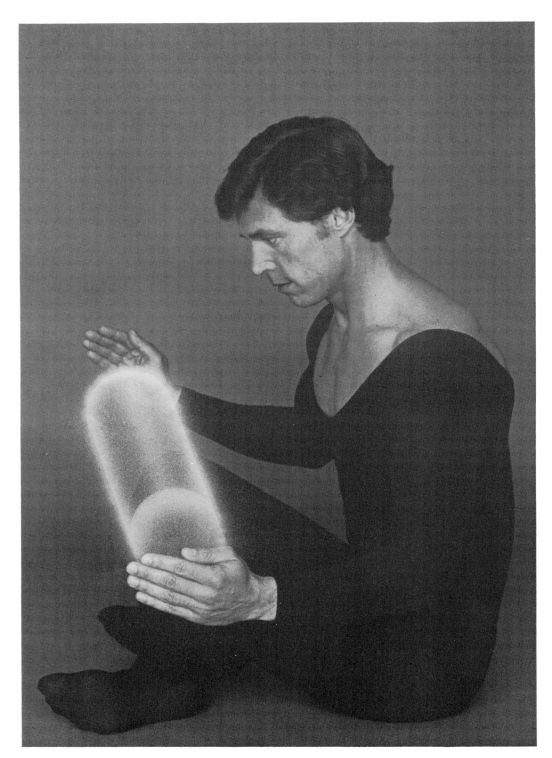

Exercise 28.1   Forming a cylinder of energy

Chapter 5

ADVANCED ENERGY PERCEPTION

You have learned both to control and to perceive energy in a variety of ways. You can direct it, read emotions carried by it, and harmonize it. In this chapter you will further increase your awareness and control of psychic energy. You will form it into shapes; you will perceive it both by using physical senses and by using psychic perception directly; and you will further develop your skill in psychometry. The tests provided in this chapter aim to give you an objective way to reinforce your confidence in your perception.

The following exercises are designed to teach you how to use your perceptual equipment; to help you discover the strengths and limits of your perception; and to give you a series of objective experiences that will build your trust in your psychic abilities. In Exercise 28: Forming Sculpted Energy, you will enhance your kinaesthetic sense and will begin working with distance perception of energy. In Exercise 30: Perceiving Clouds of Energy, you will further develop your perception. These skills will be thoroughly and objectively tested. In Exercise 32: Seeing Energy, you will develop a spectacular mode, visual perception. Finally, in Exercises 33 and 34: Advanced Psychometry, you will sharpen your ability to perceive information carried by energy, an important skill which has many practical applications.

Psychic perception comes differently for different people. In order to find your best mode of perception and develop it quickly and efficiently, supportive but accurate feedback is essential. It is hard not to fall into the error of giving emotional reassurance rather than giving honest feedback. Both are necessary, but the two should never be confused. Be scrupulously accurate. Slanted feedback prevents the full development of psychic skills. Very often the underlying reason for giving slanted feedback is that we do not firmly believe that psychic skills are a reality. However, by now you have had enough experience with psychic energy to know that it can bear your most detached examination.

EXERCISE 28.   FORMING SCULPTED ENERGY

Repetitions   Two or more for each shape.

Preparation   Clean the room psychically. Have the rock salt ready. Clean (Waterfall and Scraping). Flower to Bud. Sit opposite your partner in the Grounded Position. In this and all the other exercises in this chapter, you will need to clean the excess energy off your hands frequently. Be sure your rock salt is fresh.

Explanation   This exercise is an excellent method of developing your psychic perception. In addition, it develops your control of psychic energy and your general psychic strength.

Shaper's Instructions   Generate energy as you did in the earlier exercises. Direct the energy out of your hands and form it like clay into a small sphere about the size of a tennis ball. You may want to make a larger ball and then compact it so that the energy is very dense. Since energy is quite malleable, it is easy to shape; however, it is difficult to create an energy structure that will maintain its shape under the pressure of human touch. Therefore, you may need to add layers of energy and compact them into your sphere, making it as dense as possible. Place the sphere of energy carefully between you and your partner.

Perceiver's Instructions   Touch the sphere of energy lightly. Allow your hands to slide around its edges. Cup it carefully in both your hands. Be aware of the warmth of the energy and the weight in your hands. Did your partner make a perfect sphere, or is it asymmetrical? Press the sphere gently with a fingertip. Does it dimple in? Scatter? Toss it lightly from hand to hand. Does it retain its shape? Play with it. When you are finished, place it in the rock salt.

Conclusion   Use various geometric shapes such as cubes, cylinders, and pyramids. Change roles and repeat. Record your observations in your journal.

Variation   Perceive the energy form without touching it. What can you discern about its shape and density? Check your perception with touch.

Advanced Variation: Solidifying Energy   With practice you can learn not only to compact but to solidify energy. Solidified energy is energy which is densely compacted into a coherent shape and which has a slow, uniform vibration. To solidify an energy form completely after compacting it, you must tune it to a frequency somewhat lower than your own vibration. As before, you will want to use a colour or tone as an analogy to aid you. Keep in mind that your personal vibration is composed of a range of frequencies. The solidified energy form should be one frequency only. Choose a darker colour for the energy you want to solidify. If you use tone, choose a lower tone. As you experiment, you will find the best visualization for your needs. Repeat the above exercise using this technique to solidify the energy forms.

Exercise 28.1   Forming a cylinder of energy.

Exercise 28.2   Forming a sphere of energy.

Exercise 28.3   Forming a pyramid of energy.

EXERCISE 29. TESTING YOUR PERCEPTION OF SCULPTED ENERGY

Repetitions   Six or more.

Preparation   Clean the room psychically. Have the rock salt ready. Clean (Waterfall and Scraping). Perceiver is to leave the room and wait until called. You will then sit opposite your partner in the Grounded Position.

Explanation   This exercise will give you an opportunity to test and verify your perceptions and your skills in shaping energy into physically perceptible forms.

Shaper's Instructions   Begin by making either a cube or a sphere. Call your partner in and let him perceive the energy form. When he can easily distinguish between a cube and a sphere, you will want to add a cylinder to the range of choices. Subsequently, add a pyramid in order to develop his skill in perceiving different shapes.

Perceiver's Instructions   Touch the form, being careful not to alter its shape. Sometimes people inadvertently change the shape of the energy as they try to perceive it. Do not forget to place each form in the rock salt when you finish with it.

Conclusion   Change roles and repeat. Practise this exercise until you have sharpened your skills in shaping and perceiving energy. Record your observations in your journal.

EXERCISE 30. PERCEIVING CLOUDS OF ENERGY

Repetitions   Six or more.

Preparation   Clean the room psychically. Have the rock salt ready. Clean (Waterfall and Scraping). Flower to Bud. Sit opposite your partner in the Grounded Position.

Explanation   This exercise will help you develop the ability to perceive energy at a distance. Developing more than one mode of perception will expand your psychic range and will give you the ability to check yourself.

Shaper's Instructions   Create energy and send it out from your finger into the space between you and your partner. Send energy of as dense a quality as possible. It will form a cloud. Maintain control of the energy, adjusting the amount as needed to keep the cloud intact throughout the exercise.

Perceiver's Instructions   Sense the energy without touching it. Just as you learned in the earlier exercises, some people perceive energy with visual images, others with sound, others kinaesthetically. Open your perceptions. Are you aware, without touching it, of the energy your partner has generated between you? Does the space between you seem crowded? Is it lighter or darker than other space? When you have a sense of the shape of the energy between you and your partner, touch it to check your first perception.

Exercise 30.1   Checking perception of an energy cloud.

Exercise 30.2   Bumping energy clouds.

Shaper's Instructions   Now slowly take the energy from the cloud back into your body. Clean your hands.

Perceiver's Instructions   Can you see the cloud diminish? Can you sense that there is less energy between you and your partner? Is the air calmer, quieter? Use your hand to check. Clean your hands as necessary for clear perception.

Conclusion   Change roles and repeat. Record your observations in your journal.

Variation   This variation uses kinaesthetic perception. Both partners will form separate energy clouds simultaneously. You may wish to make these smaller and more compact than the ones you made earlier. Push the clouds together. Be aware of the pressure on your hand as your partner's cloud pushes against yours.

EXERCISE 31.   TESTING YOUR PERCEPTION OF CLOUDS OF ENERGY

Repetitions   Six or more.

Preparation   Clean the room psychically. Have the rock salt ready. Clean (Waterfall and Scraping). Flower to Bud. Sit opposite your partner in the Grounded Position.

Shaper's Instructions   You will form an energy cloud and alternately increase and decrease its dimensions. Write down your sequence before you begin. Your list might look like this: Increase, Decrease, Increase, Increase, Decrease. Inform your partner as you begin each change. Practising this exercise will aid in developing his energy perception.

Perceiver's Instructions   Use your new perceptual sense to discern whether the energy in the area between you and your partner is increasing or decreasing. You may check by touch if necessary. When you are finished, scrape the excess energy from your hands into the rock salt.

Conclusion   Change roles and repeat. Clean the room psychically. Record your observations in your journal.

Trouble-shooting   Keep in mind that this is a difficult exercise and that you are developing a new perception. If it took you some weeks to feel clearly energy moving into your hand in Exercise 1: Exchanging Energy, you should anticipate that this exercise will take at least as much time. It is also an exercise that frequently gives rise to self doubt. Be objective, methodical, and patient.

EXERCISE 32. SEEING ENERGY

Repetitions   This exercise is to be done in five-minute sets of no more than thirty minutes' total duration.

Preparation   Clean the room psychically. Have the rock salt ready. Clean (Waterfall and Scraping). Flower to Bud. Sit opposite your partner in the Grounded Position. This exercise can be done alone or with a partner.

Explanation   Just as it is possible to feel energy with your physical body, so it is possible, given the right circumstances, to see energy physically. To do this you need a dark room, since energy is most readily visible against a dark background. Be sure the room has been well cleaned. Too much random energy will interfere with your perception.

Sender's Instructions   Generate energy and form a globe in the centre of your body. Direct the energy down your arm and out of all four fingers, upward towards the ceiling. Spread your fingers, then close them. Do this slowly several times. While you are opening and closing your fingers, project different variations of energy. You may want to go up and down the spectrum or musical scale. Some vibrations are more readily perceptible than others, and simply changing vibrations will make seeing the energy easier. Clean your hands as necessary.

Perceiver's Instructions   No special effort of the eyes is needed. It is not

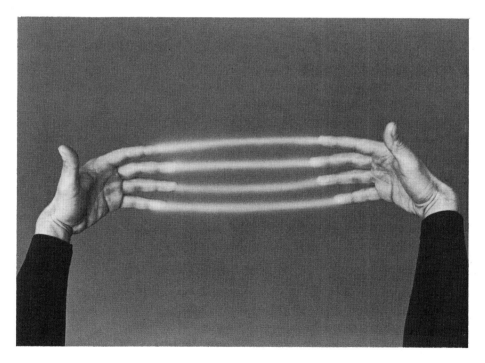

Exercise 32.1   Seeing energy.

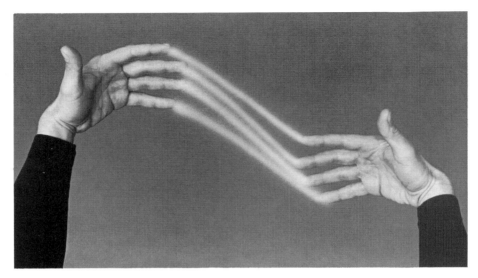

Exercise 32.2   Seeing energy — variation.

necessary to stare or strain. When you are successful you will see white streaks, vapour, or sparks of energy.

Conclusion   Change roles and repeat. Record your observations in your journal.

Trouble-shooting   Physically seeing psychic energy is dramatic and can be useful, but keep in mind that reliable perception does not depend on physical sight. The goal of perceptual exercises is to help you find and develop your own most natural mode of psychic perception.

Remember, as we have said before, that it is important that your best perceptive mode, whatever it is, becomes familiar and reliable. Just as in other aspects of life, you should work with your natural bent. If your orientation is kinaesthetic, concentrate on developing that sense. If energy comes as tone, work with that. You will want to develop a secondary means of perception to balance and to confirm your first, but you should emphasize your strongest mode.

Variation A   Direct energy from one hand to the other through your finger tips. Move your hands to cause the energy to flow diagonally; then move them slowly back to the straight position. Again, you may wish to go up and down the scale. Maintain a relaxed alertness. Be careful not to exhaust yourself by working too long. When you complete the exercise, clean (Waterfall and Scraping). You may also want to exchange energy with nature. Later, when you are rested, clean the room again.

Variation B   Sit facing your partner in a darkened room. Generate energy. Place your fingers about four inches from his. You and your partner will send concentrated energy to each other from your fingers. Gradually move your fingers in order to make observation of the energy easier.

EXERCISE 33. ADVANCED PSYCHOMETRY (GENERAL READING)

Repetitions Six or more.

Preparation Have the rock salt ready. Clean (Waterfall and Scraping). Flower to Bud. Sit opposite your partner in the Grounded Position.

Explanation Psychometry is the art of reading detailed information from the energy carried by an object. You have already learned a basic form of psychometry in Exercise 17. Because our energy carries all kinds of information about us, there is a wide variety of information available to be read. The information is there; the skill to read it can be acquired.

Enquirer's Instructions Give your partner an article of jewellery that you have worn for some time. Do not psychically clean the jewellery. If the object has been cleaned, there will be no energy on it for your partner to read.

Reader's Instructions Hold the article of jewellery loosely in your hand. Rub your fingers lightly across it to get a sense of your partner's energy. You may want to tune yourself slightly to this vibration. Relax and focus on your perceptions. If images come to your mind, describe them. If you sense something through direct perception, say it. It is probable that the images or feelings will not make sense. Logic belongs to your linear mind and in this exercise you use the non-linear part of your consciousness which is oriented to images and emotions. Often seemingly unlikely perceptions are quite accurate. Of course, ideas or events may present themselves symbolically. One of the aims of this exercise is for the Reader to attain familiarity with his own symbolic alphabet. As always, be aware that you are developing a new skill, and be patient with yourself.

Enquirer's Instructions Since both of you are trying to develop an understanding of the way your individual psychic perceptions work, it is important for the person who has the Enquirer's role to make clear, methodical notes, and to give accurate, positive feedback. Have your notebook ready. Some people prefer to have the Enquirer interject feedback during the reading, while others find that this interrupts their concentration. Either way, the Enquirer must be scrupulously honest. Never indicate that something is true if it is not. Never pretend to understand what you do not. A positive attitude is necessary; accurate, honest feedback is essential. Remember that you are helping the Reader to develop a new skill, not simply giving him reassurance. No athlete, no actor, no singer would ever develop mastery of his craft if he were guided by an admiring disciple rather than a coach.

Conclusion Change roles and repeat. Clean your hands between readings. Synthesize and record your notes in your journal.

Trouble-shooting Psychic reading is an art form. If six artists paint the same scene, six different paintings are created; if six Readers read for the same Enquirer, each will focus on a different aspect of the person or his situation. The medium with which you interpret the information is your own mind, and the information that you perceive is necessarily filtered through your own view of the world. What you perceive, as well as the manner in which you perceive it, is therefore dictated largely by your deeply held assumptions about the nature of reality. During a reading, a selection process takes place. The Reader focuses on information that he feels is important, relevant, or interesting. Other kinds of information are generally disregarded. In ordinary interactions, if you ask two people to tell you about a mutual friend, one may talk about how much money the friend makes, and the other may talk about what kinds of jokes he tells. Both are being honest; both are correct; but the details they select are determined by their personal ideas of what is important. So it is with psychic Readers.

Obviously, to be a good Reader requires an open mind and a flexible view of the world. A constricted mind can only have a constricted view, and can only give a limited and essentially useless reading.

Advanced Variation: Field Work   In order to sharpen your skills and to provide a greater range for your development as a reader, you will want to practise psychometry with many different people. Ask your partner to bring an article of jewellery from another person whom he knows well and you do not. Practise with various friends – people you can rely on for honest feedback. You may even wish to practise with someone that you are only slightly acquainted with, or perhaps with a stranger.

EXERCISE 34.   ADVANCED PSYCHOMETRY (SPECIFIC READING)

Repetitions   Six or more.

Preparation   Have the rock salt ready. Clean (Waterfall and Scraping). Flower to Bud. Sit opposite your partner in the Grounded Position.

Explanation   The filtering process of the mind allows the Reader consciously to select information. In this exercise you will read in response to direct questions.

Enquirer's Instructions   Ask a specific question that relates to a current event in your life or to something in the immediate past. Examples are:

'What is the current situation regarding ...?'
'What are ...'s motives regarding ...?'
'Why did ... occur?' (Or why not?)
'What is causing ...?'
'... event has just occurred. Please describe what you perceive about it.'

Reader's Instructions   Hold the jewellery loosely in your hand. Relax. Breathe deeply and evenly. Repeat the question slowly over and over with the assurance that the answer is there and you can find it. Do not take refuge in your conscious knowledge and opinions. They are very likely wrong. This is an exercise that takes a certain kind of courage. Be brave. Relax. Trust yourself. Trust your partner. Articulate the perceptions that come to you.

Enquirer's Instructions Again, keep methodical notes and give accurate feedback.

Conclusion Change roles and repeat. Clean your hands between readings. Record your observations in your journal.

Trouble-shooting Over a period of time you will begin to see which kinds of information are easiest for you and your partner to read. One of you may focus more easily on emotional issues; the other on questions of finance or health. As always, develop your strengths until they are reliable, and then begin to work on your weaknesses.

Advanced Variation: Field Work Repeat the Advanced Variation from Exercise 33, focusing on specific questions.

Daily Training
Practise the following exercises daily, in this sequence:
Exercises 10: Waterfall and 11: Scraping
Exercise 16: Calisthenics: Flower to Bud
Exercise 22: Tuning to Yourself
Exercise 6: Calisthenics: Flowing Energy Through Your Entire Body, Variation

Exercise 35   Draining another person's energy.

Chapter 6

PSYCHIC SELF-DEFENCE

The purpose of psychic self-defence is to enable you to increase safely your psychic sensitivity. Although we will be teaching you how to build psychic weapons, please understand that they are meant to be used only as aids in improving your defences. We do not condone psychic violence any more than we condone physical violence. Those of us who are more knowledgeable in the area of psychic skills than others are have a particular obligation to observe high ethical behaviour. After some debate, we have included this chapter because we cannot in conscience teach you to increase your psychic perception and sensitivity without also showing you how to improve your defences. Overt psychic attack is rare, but having to contend with a barrage of negative energy, or with energy drain, is common. This two-part chapter will prepare you to defend yourself against energy drain, negative energy, and overt psychic attack.

Part One: Energy Drain
Energy interchange is a normal, healthy aspect of any relationship. As in other aspects of relationships, the exchange should be fairly equal. However, it sometimes happens that people drain one another even without consciously intending harm. People do not have to know anything about psychic energy to drain you.

A friend who is going through an illness or a difficult emotional situation, such as a divorce, may drain your energy simply because, on a subconscious level, he confuses energy with emotional support. It is important, therefore, for you to learn how to defend yourself against this process. It also happens that you may unknowingly send too much energy to certain people. Perhaps you feel that a person is dependent on you; perhaps you feel guilty; or perhaps you see him as needing your help in some way. You may send large amounts of energy in his direction in response to your feelings. In fact, energy sent in this way will not help the person, may actually be harmful to him, and will surely deplete you. If you question that this energy may be harmful to him, remember what you felt when you absorbed a relatively small amount of untuned energy (Exercise 24). Psychic energy is physical. It may carry emotion, but it is not emotion. Likewise, it is possible to give emotional support without draining your own energy. This emotional support is what is needed. Indeed, sending small amounts of tuned energy that are highly charged with love and acceptance is much better for both of you than your being drained of large, indiscriminate quantities of untuned energy. Bear in mind that all of us have tremendous reserves of psychic energy at our disposal, both from the environment around us and from the generating power of our own bodies. We do not need to drain other people's energy. In spite of this abundance of energy, many people experience energy drain with its accompanying symptoms of fatigue and lethargy. In fact, energy drain can cause a variety of physical and emotional problems. You have learned to take energy from nature and to generate energy, so you can replenish yourself under most circumstances. However, you also need to learn how to prevent energy drain. Learning to stop energy drain before it becomes a severe problem is the purpose of these exercises.

EXERCISE 35. EXPERIENCING ENERGY DRAIN

Repetitions One.

Preparation Have the rock salt ready. Clean (Waterfall and Scraping). The Taker will sit in the Grounded Position.

Explanation Because energy drain is usually a gradual process, and because the symptoms of being energy drained can be subtle and will vary from person to person, it is important to experience energy drain under controlled conditions. By taking your energy, your partner is helping you learn to build good defences. When you have learned your body's symptoms, it will be easy for you to discern when you are being drained and to take proper defensive action. Once you have fully and consciously experienced energy drain, your body will react to it very quickly and your defence against it will become automatic.

Perceiver's Instructions Lie in a relaxed position on your back, feet apart, arms at your sides. Breathe slowly and evenly and focus your awareness on your energy-body. You may wish to compare your sensations with those you experienced when your partner was taking energy from you in Exercise 2. You will need to keep him informed as to your sensations.

Taker's Instructions Take energy liberally from your partner, using both hands. Deposit the energy in the rock salt, being careful not to absorb it yourself. Take energy from several different areas of your partner's body. Continue for five minutes or more. You and the Perceiver will be able to determine between you when he has a clear perception of the sensations of energy drain. Keep a log of the Perceiver's responses.

Conclusion Clean (Waterfall and Scraping). Record your observations in your

Exercise 35   Draining another person's energy.

journal. In order to allow the Perceiver to regain his full strength, it will be necessary to wait three or four days before changing roles.

Trouble-shooting   Most people feel very tired after being drained. However, symptoms vary. You may feel dizzy, weak, nauseous, irritable, or depressed. You may be less well co-ordinated than usual. These symptoms will pass in a day or two. We have found that the more uncomfortable a student's experience is, the better his later defence will be. However, be careful when driving, and take it easy for a while.

Do not ask your partner to give you energy. Do not even generate energy or take energy from nature. You must not deliberately increase your energy at all because it occasionally happens that some of the energy channels will collapse after energy drain. Although they will relax and reopen of their own accord, forcing energy into them can cause damage. If after two days you are still tired and lethargic, perform Exercise 36: Bud to Flower.

Occasionally it happens that a person will actually feel better after experiencing energy drain. This indicates that he had an excess of energy in his body, and draining off some of this excess energy has resulted in an improvement in his energy flow. People who have this experience will benefit from regular practice of Exercise 6: Flowing Energy Through Your Entire Body and from Exercise 8: Exchanging Energy with Nature, being careful never to draw in more energy than they send out.

EXERCISE 36. SOLO EXERCISE: FIRST AID FOR COLLAPSED CHANNELS (BUD TO FLOWER)

Repetitions   As needed.

Preparation   Clean (Waterfall and Scraping). Ideally this exercise should be performed lying down on the grass.

Explanation   The object of this exercise is to help you open and relax channels that have collapsed due to energy drain. Opening the collapsed channels will enable your energy-body to draw in energy from the surrounding environment at its own pace. It is extremely important that you be very gentle in your practice of this exercise, and that you do not consciously draw in energy. Allow your body's natural rhythms of energy flow to resume at their own speed.

Instructions   Visualize that your right hand is a tight bud. Open it gently into a full flower. Continue the opening process all the way up your arm to your shoulder. Repeat with your left arm; then go through the same process, first with your right leg, then with your left. Next, open your torso, moving upwards gradually, and ending with your head.

Conclusion   Observe your sensations immediately after performing this exercise, one hour later, and the next day. Record your observations in your journal.

Energy Channels

Energy channels correspond in great measure to acupuncture meridians. Any acupuncturist will say that the channels he works with to affect the physical body are only a few of the many meridians that exist in it. Although even the science of acupuncture does not classify or fully understand all of these other channels, our research indicates that many of them are the physical structures within the energy-body that are used in psychic work. When any kind of energy interchange takes place, the energy flows along these channels. To protect against energy drain, one must stop the flow of energy out of these channels. This can be done by forcing the channels to close so that they do not carry energy. Your body will do this if the energy drain becomes critical, by causing the channels actually to collapse. However, collapsed channels are uncomfortable and can also be dangerous. This is an energy-body process analogous to going into shock.

A lesser version of this trauma occurs when excess energy collects within the channels and coalesces to form blocks. As we have indicated, energy channels collapse only under extreme conditions of being deliberately drained from outside. On the other hand, we all inadvertently form energy blocks from time to time in response to ordinary stresses such as pain or fear. Since we all do this, it is a good idea to practise Exercise 6: Flowing Energy Through Your Entire Body regularly in order to clear out energy blocks.

Fortunately, you can consciously stop the energy flow in several ways. It may be stopped by physically protecting the main valves through which energy flows, or by building a barrier between yourself and the sources of the energy drain.

EXERCISE 37. FIELD WORK: SECURE POSITION (LESSENING ENERGY DRAIN)

Repetitions   As needed.

Explanation   The main energy exit points are: the soles of the feet, the palms of the hands, the chest, the pelvis, the head, and the two large meridians which bisect the body vertically. By assuming the secure position, you can protect the major exit points in the hands, the feet, and the pelvis. This simple posture will materially slow energy drain. It is designed to be used when you are in public, have no time for preparation, and realize that your energy is being drained.

Instructions   Clasp your hands together with your thumbs on the outside. Do not interlock your fingers. Hold your clasped hands, palm to palm, in front of you on your lap. Keep your legs together and your feet flat on the floor.

Exercise 37   Secure position.

EXERCISE 38.   BUILDING A BARRIER

Repetitions   Six or more.

Preparation   Clean (Waterfall and Scraping). Flower to Bud. Stand in the Grounded Position.

Explanation   Building a barrier, in addition to teaching you a protective measure, also develops two very important psychic skills. The first skill is learning to manipulate energy by using only visualization and the energy-body. The second skill is solidifying energy forms – a technique you were introduced to in Exercise 28.

It is important to remember that when you manipulate energy by visualization you are not manipulating it by the power of your imagination. The strength of your entire energy-body is used in this exercise. It will create and maintain the barrier that you visualize. You will not need to make any physical motions in order to create and maintain the barrier. The ability to build successfully through visualization and to perceive accurately what you have built is the reward of your steady practice of psychic skills and of the honest feedback you and your partner have been giving each other all along.

Builder's Instructions   Generate and project energy. Visualize a wall between yourself and your partner (later, between yourself and the person you suspect of draining your energy). This image should be as specific and vivid as you can possibly make it. You may wish to visualize a wall of brick, of stone, of plate

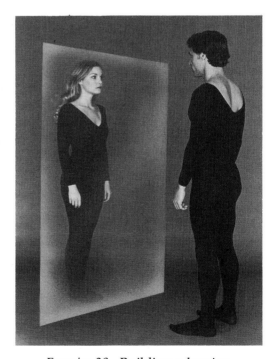

Exercise 38   Building a barrier.

glass, or of steel. Project energy as you visualize the barrier. Visualize the wall so clearly that you can see it, feel it, and hear how it affects sound. Then stop projecting; solidify and release the wall. Be careful not to dissolve the wall when you release it.

As you know, thoughts and emotions are continuously projected by energy. When you visualize the wall, your energy-body projects a thought form. As you clarify and strengthen that image, your energy-body clarifies and strengthens the form. Instruct your energy-body to solidify the form. Tune the energy to a slow uniform vibration, as you did in Exercise 28. Forming Sculpted Energy (Advanced Variation). If you have done this successfully, the completed energy barrier will be clearly discernible, dense, and well shaped. At the end of the exercise, dissolve the barrier either by changing its uniform frequency to many disparate ones, or by using a dissonant frequency to shatter it.

Perceiver's Instructions   Touch the wall. Determine its thickness and solidity. Is it closer to the Builder than he intended? Further away? Is it the same thickness throughout its length, or are there gaps?

The feedback that you give to your partner enables him to direct his energy better. He will, by responding to your feedback, not only learn how to create barriers better but, more importantly, will learn to direct his energy-body and non-linear mind better. They will, in turn, become more responsive as the commands become clearer and more frequent. As always, be as honest as you can.

Conclusion   Change roles and repeat. Clean the room psychically. Record your observations in your journal.

Advanced Variation   You may wish to use a barrier to block negative energy that is being directed towards you or another person. If you are tuning to someone in a public place, you may need to make a barrier to prevent interference.

EXERCISE 39.   SOLO EXERCISE: CLOSING ENERGY CONNECTIONS

Repetitions   As needed.
Preparation   Clean (Waterfall and Scraping). Flower to Bud.
Explanation   It occasionally happens that people drain your energy even though they are many miles away from you. As with most types of energy drain, these people generally are not aware that they are draining your energy, and they have no desire to hurt you. In fact, these are probably the people most interested in your well-being. You are sure to have a strong emotional and psychic connection with anyone who drains you in this way. Probably a person draining you from a distance is in need of emotional support or some other kind of interchange with you. The interchange he needs, whatever it may be, should not drain your energy. Keep in mind that we give each other emotional support all the time without ever having to deplete our vital forces.

Also, remember what too much untuned energy can do to the person who absorbs it.

Psychic connections between people are complex. This exercise employs a simple image – a symbol – to represent the psychic energy connections between people. In this exercise you will close the energy links through which you are being drained. These are only energy connections, not emotional ties.

Those of you who are in the service professions may find that your clients or students are draining you. Other people should look first to family and close friends.

Instructions   Lie down in a comfortable position. Visualize clear plastic tubes extending from different places on your body which reach out to connect with the various people in your life. Gradually close these tubes. Visualize them getting smaller. When you have closed all the tubes, relax, build strength, and tune to yourself before getting up.

Conclusion   Record your observations in your journal.

Trouble-shooting   If you feel better after having done this exercise, you were probably being drained. The tubes will re-open. Therefore, if you are subject to energy drain, you should do this exercise periodically.

Advanced Variation: Diagnosis   After you have closed the links, you will open them again one at a time. Be alert to your sensations as you carefully re-establish each link. You experienced energy drain in Exercise 35. Do you now feel the same sensation as you re-establish any tie? If you do, you must keep that connection closed. You should check it twice a day until the problem of energy drain has stopped.

Part Two: Shields and Weapons
You have now attained considerable mastery in controlling energy. You can send it, take it, shape it, and solidify it. Now you can use your skills to build devices for the protection of yourself or another person. In learning to build shields, you not only learn a skill that will protect you from energy drain and psychic attack, and that will keep you clean when you are in a dirty environment, but you also learn an effective method for developing energy-body strength, since the construction of psychic shields is itself a strength-building exercise. Because building a shield stresses each part of the energy-body equally, it also aids in removing energy blocks and congestion, thus developing energy-body clarity. When you visualize the shields in the following exercises, remember that by visualizing you are not simply imagining. Rather, you are giving your energy-body instructions through images.

A psychic shield is a more advanced and complex form of the energy barrier that you learned earlier. It is the best defence against both energy drain and psychic attack because it allows no energy to enter or leave your body. For this reason, it will also prevent natural healthy interchange of energy with your environment. Therefore, you will not want to wear your shield constantly and, of course, you cannot wear your shield if you wish to tune or give energy.

Ideally your shield will be no more than a quarter of an inch thick. A heavy shield is difficult to hold up for any length of time and is apt to crack under its own weight. As you become more advanced, your shield will become thinner still, until it is a second skin of impermeable energy. The ideal shield is lightweight, strong, flexible, and fitted evenly over the entire body.

EXERCISE 40.   THE BUBBLE SHIELD

Repetitions   Six or more.

Preparation   Clean (Waterfall and Scraping). Flower to Bud. Stand in the Grounded Position.

Explanation   The Bubble Shield is easy to make and is an excellent protection against psychic attack, energy drain, and psychic dirt. It may be that you will have to make shields under conditions of stress, and you may not be able to perform the complete Preparation. In that case, you must rely entirely on the Grounded Position to give you the strength that you need. At the earliest opportunity, you should clean, exchange energy with nature, and tune to yourself.

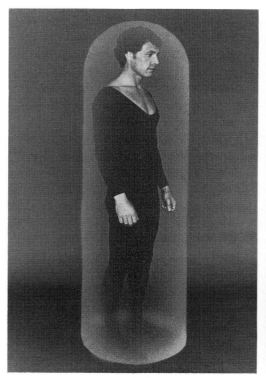

Exercise 40.1 Psychic shield.   *Exercise 40.2* Unsuccessful bubble shield.

Exercise 40.3   Find the outer boundary of a shield.

Exercise 40.4
Determining the thickness of a shield.

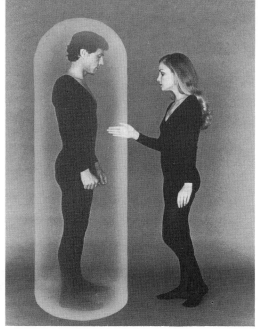

Exercise 40.5
Determining the thickness of a shield.

Shielder's Instructions Generate and project energy as you clearly visualize yourself surrounded by a capsule or bubble. You will need to see it very clearly in your mind's eye. Be sure that it goes under your feet completely; that it goes evenly up your legs; that it covers your hips; and that it is not thicker or thinner at any point. Maintain the same level of thickness over your back, chest, and arms, and be sure that the shield covers the top of your head. Go over your shield again seeing that it covers your whole body evenly. Visualize the energy coalescing to become very solid, yet light and flexible (see Exercise 28, Advanced Variation: Solidifying Energy). When you have solidified your shield, ask your partner to give you feedback. Once you have mastered the energy-solidifying technique, your shield will maintain itself with little attention until you take it down.

Perceiver's Instructions To find the outer boundary of your partner's shield, start at some distance from his body and gradually move forward. When you touch the shield, you may perceive an electric tingling, or a slight resistance. When you have found the outside boundary, let your hands slide up and down the shield wall to discern its outlines.

Now determine the thickness of the shield. Find its inner boundary. Place your hand, palm outward, against your partner's body. Slowly bring your hand outward until you reach the inner shield wall. Is the back of the shield the same thickness as the front? Check at several points. Now place your hand through the shield so that you are aware of its inner and outer boundaries at the same time. You may feel a pressure on your hand. This will indicate the thickness of the shield. When your partner has mastered the Bubble Shield, there will be little or no variation in thickness.

Describe your perception of the shield to your partner. How well has he been able to manifest his visualization? Did he cover his feet? His head? His hands? His hips? The backs of his knees? Check the back of his neck, the top of his head, his eyes, and his ears. If there are holes in his shield, you can find them by gently taking energy with your hand. If you can successfully draw energy from him at any spot, then he must strengthen his shield at that point. Of course, if you put your hand inside his shield, you will be able to take his energy. You must be outside the shield to check it. If you can draw energy from the shield itself, it has not been properly solidified.

Conclusion Dissolve the shield. Change roles and repeat. Clean the room psychically. Record your observations in your journal.

Advanced Variation When you are comfortable with your shield, you should test it further. Ask your partner to talk to you and try to distract you while you are wearing your shield. How well can you maintain it? Wear it in public. Does it move with you? What do you observe as to how it affects you and your interaction with other people? Does the protection from dirt make your work easier? Does the insulation from other people's energy make communication more difficult? How long are you able to wear it comfortably?

EXERCISE 41. TESTING YOUR SHIELD AGAINST ENERGY DRAIN

Repetitions   One or two.

Preparation   Clean (Waterfall and Scraping). Flower to Bud. Stand in the Grounded Position. Work in a psychically clean environment, outside if possible.

Explanation   You have learned a position for slowing energy drain. When you have mastered the effective building of a shield, you will be able to avoid being drained by the people in your vicinity. In this exercise you will test the strength of your psychic shield against energy drain.

Defender's Instructions   Build your best shield. Let your partner know when you are ready.

Taker's Instructions   As in all of these testing situations, the best thing you can do for your partner is to do your worst. When your partner is ready, find the outer boundary of his shield so that you can stay outside it. Use your hands to go over his entire shield, trying to drain energy. Pay particular attention to any areas that were vulnerable in the last exercise, and drain there if you can.

Conclusion   Change roles and repeat. Record your observations in your journal.

Defender's Trouble-shooting   Exercise your perception. Is your partner draining your energy? If so, you left a gap in your shield. If you have built well he cannot drain you, no matter how he tries. If you have to expend energy to maintain your shield, your partner is draining the shield itself. This means you did not solidify it adequately. Practise regularly until you have mastered making a shield.

EXERCISE 42.   TESTING YOUR SHIELD WITH ENERGY FORMS

Repetitions   One or two.

Preparation   Clean (Waterfall and Scraping). Flower to Bud. Stand in the Grounded Position. Work outdoors if possible.

Explanation   Testing your shield by throwing concentrated energy forms at it will enable you to strengthen it. When your shield can stand up to this concentrated direct attack, it will easily be able to withstand the unformed negative energy you ordinarily have to deal with.

Defender's Instructions   Make your shield.

Shaper's Instructions   Build an energy sphere (Exercise 28). Be sure you have it compressed and solidified. Throw it vigorously at your partner. You may even work from behind him.

Do this several times. How well does your sphere hold up? Does it flatten?

Does it disintegrate? Is your partner's shield able to stand up to your best effort?

Conclusion Change roles and repeat. Clean thoroughly. If you have been working indoors, clean the room. Place any remaining energy forms in the rock salt.

Defender's Trouble-shooting Could you feel your friend's energy sphere strike your shield? Did your shield crack? If so, it is too thick or too brittle. Did your partner make a hole in your shield? If so, your shield needs to be better solidified.

Advanced Variation When both of your shields can withstand these attacks, change the shapes of your weapons. Try lances or darts. Use your imagination. How well does the shield stand up to the new weapons?

Exercise 42.1 Advanced variation — making a dart.

Exercise 42.2   Advanced variation — testing a shield.

Exercise 42.3   Advanced variation — locating a dart.

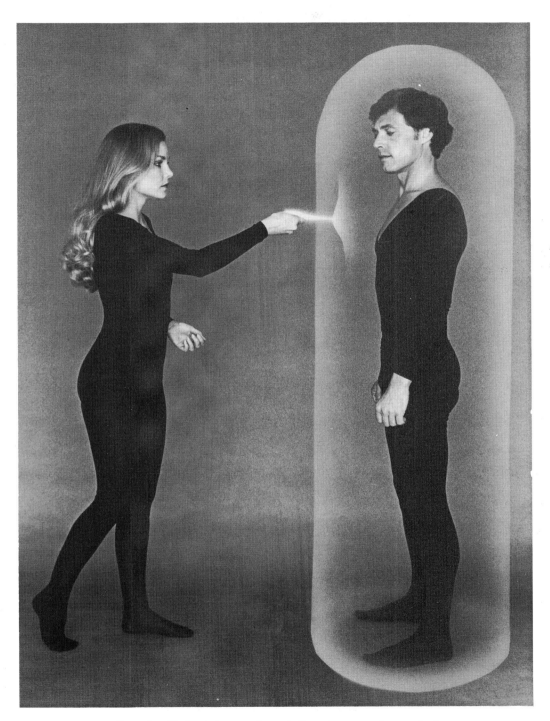

Exercise 42.4   Advanced variation — removing a dart.

Exercise 42.5 Advanced variation — testing a dart.

After testing the shield, you will have to remove any weapons that remain in it. Check the shield carefully. When you find a weapon, remove it and dispose of it in the rock salt. If you are working indoors, you will need to find and dispose of any weapons that may have fallen on the floor. If a weapon actually penetrates the shield and strikes you, be sure to remove it as well as any particles of foreign or solidified energy. Clean the wounded area carefully.

EXERCISE 43. SOLO EXERCISE: TESTING THE STRENGTH OF YOUR WEAPONS

Repetitions One.

Preparation Have the rock salt ready. Clean (Waterfall and Scraping). Flower to Bud.

Explanation Before utilizing psychic weapons you must understand exactly the damage they can do. Very often people have an exaggerated notion of how dangerous they are. While it is true that psychic energy is physical and that psychic weapons will affect your body, they are usually much less harmful than many people seem to think. To find out exactly how dangerous your psychic weapons are, you must test them.

Instructions Make a dart. Make it very solid. Then, with all your strength, thrust the dart into your own hand. Be aware of your sensations. Let the dart remain in your hand for a brief period. What happens? Remove the dart, and place it in the rock salt. Carefully clean your hand. Draw out any alien energy. Check your sensations the next day. Has your hand healed, or is it still wounded? Now you know the extent of the damage you can do.

Trouble-shooting Students often experience a throbbing or dull ache after testing their darts. This will soon diminish and disappear since the energy-body heals itself readily. It is important to keep the area clean to facilitate the healing process.

Conclusion Record your observations in your journal.

Variation You may want to test your weapons more completely. What is the effect if you do not remove the dart for some time? What effect do your partner's weapons have on you?

EXERCISE 44. SHIELDING ANOTHER PERSON

Repetitions Six or more.

Preparation Clean (Waterfall and Scraping). Flower to Bud. Stand in the Grounded Position.

Explanation You built an energy barrier to protect another person in Exercise 38, Advanced Variation. Now you can build a shield to protect another person.

Protector's Instructions Build a shield around your partner just as you did around yourself in Exercise 40. Generate energy. Visualize your design clearly and in detail. Project energy and solidify the shield. Be sure to make the shield light as well as strong. Find its inner and outer boundaries. How well did you manifest your image? Check for gaps. Can you maintain the shield as your partner moves? Do not allow the size or density of the shield to vary. How long can you maintain it?

Perceiver's Instructions Exercise your perception as your partner builds a shield around you. If you feel hot or claustrophobic, then the shield is too small and you must ask him to make it bigger. Does one side feel heavier than the other? If so, ask him to adjust it. Does the shield move with you when you sit down? Can you walk in it? Give your partner feedback so that he can improve his skill.

Conclusion Dissolve the shield. Change roles and repeat. Clean the room psychically. Record your observations in your journal.

Advanced Variation In the future, when this exercise becomes easy, you will want to build a shield around yourself also, so that both of you are protected at once. First, build the shield around your partner and check it carefully; then build your own shield. Can you maintain both? Can you sit while your partner walks and still maintain both shields? Can your partner move out of sight and still be protected?

EXERCISE 45. SHIELDING ANOTHER PERSON TO PROTECT YOURSELF

Repetitions   Six or more.

Preparation   Clean (Waterfall and Scraping). Flower to Bud. Stand in the Grounded Position. Work outdoors if possible.

Explanation   It is easier and more effective to put a shield around a person who is attacking you than to return the attack. If you make the shield well, he will be unable to psychically harm you or anyone else, and he will experience his own negative energy.

Attacker's Instructions   Generate as much hostile energy as possible. If you choose, you may even use psychic weapons. Remember, as we said before, in order to give your partner a good opportunity to perfect his defences, it is your responsibility to try to duplicate the worst he can possibly meet.

Defender's Instructions   Visualize a shield around your partner as you did in the previous exercise. You will need to practise making this shield several times, asking your partner to step up his attack until you are able to shield an attacking person effectively. Be sure that the shield is light. If you make it too heavy it will not move with him and will not serve as an effective defence. Make it strong enough to prevent the negative energy cutting through it. With so much bad energy coming from your partner, you may find it easier to make the shield somewhat larger than before.

Conclusion   Change roles and repeat. When you have finished this exercise, you will want to clean thoroughly. If you have been working indoors, you must also clean the room. Record your observations in your journal.

EXERCISE 46.   CALISTHENICS: ENERGY SPHERES

Repetitions   Do this exercise daily.

Preparation   Clean (Waterfall and Scraping). Flower to Bud. Stand in the Grounded Position. Before you do these calisthenics, you should have been practising Exercise 6: Flowing Energy Through the Entire Body, for about six months as part of your daily training.

Explanation   This exercise is designed to strengthen and balance the energy-body and to dissolve energy blocks.

Instructions   Form energy spheres in your body in the following places and in this order: feet, knees, groin, the centre of the body, heart area, shoulders, elbows, hands, lower throat, upper throat and the top of the head. Try to keep all the spheres the same size. It may be some weeks before you can maintain them all evenly. When you can maintain all the different spheres at one time you are ready to move on to the Advanced Variation of this exercise.

Advanced Variation   Build all the spheres as before. Radiate energy gently and evenly from both spheres in the feet. At the same time, keep all the other spheres stable in shape, place, and size. When you have radiated energy from the spheres in your feet, bring the energy back in and return the spheres to their original size. Now repeat, radiating energy from the spheres in your knees while you hold all the other spheres stable. Absorb the energy that you radiated outwards and proceed, radiating energy from each sphere, or pair of spheres, in sequence.

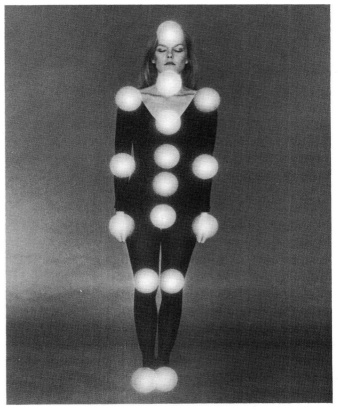

Exercise 46   Energy spheres.

Daily Training
Practise the following exercises daily, in this sequence:
Exercises 10: Waterfall and 11: Scraping
Exercise 16: Calisthenics: Flower to Bud
Exercise 22: Tuning to Yourself
Exercise 46: Calisthenics: Energy Spheres

Chapter 7

GROUP EXERCISES

You will find practising your new skills with a group of people helpful in many ways. Working with a group of people will introduce you to many kinds of energy and to many modes of perception. Since each person's psychic perceptions operate somewhat differently, working with several people will allow you to develop a wider range of perception. In addition, a group provides a variety of reinforcement and feedback, and a group can also perform a wide variety of experiments. You can learn much from each other's different perceptions and experiences. Besides, working in a group is simply more fun.

These exercises are written with from three to ten people in mind. They are based on the techniques of the previous chapters. Any group exercise can be done whenever all the members have learned the techniques related to that exercise.

EXERCISE 47. CLEANING A ROOM

Repetitions Perform the Wind Visualization before doing any psychic work as a group. Do the Scraping as needed.

Reference See Exercise 13: Cleaning a Room

Preparation Open the doors and windows. Stand in the Grounded Position. One of you will read the Wind Visualization aloud so that the group can work in unison.

Explanation Since rooms where many people work build up a great deal of psychic dirt quickly, it is wise to clean a room both before and after any psychic work.

Cleaners' Instructions, Wind Visualization You will focus your energy-bodies and use your energy to move a physical substance: psychic dirt. To do this, vividly visualize a great wind sweeping past you and blowing the stale energy out through the door. Visualize the wind as a tremendous force – a huge gale that sweeps through the room taking all the dirty energy in its path and pushing it out through the doors and windows. Be aware of it blowing through the entire room, floor to ceiling. Feel the force of the wind moving past you. Listen to the sound as it blows through the whole room. Visualize the wind blowing all the dirty energy out of the corners. Because of its force, the wind moves dirt from places you cannot even see: from behind the bookcase, from under the couch. Be aware of the wind as it blows the old energy from the rug, from the skirting-boards, the walls, the door frames, the curtains, the windows themselves, the lamps and lampshades, and from deep within the furniture. Be aware of the cool, clean wind blowing throughout the room. Smell the crisp, fresh air the wind brings.

Cleaners' Instructions, Scraping Just as you need to scrape heavy energy off your body, you will want to scrape the heavy energy out of the room. Find the places where people sit most often; these will be the places that have the most static energy. Begin in the Grounded Position. Then move through the room, scraping the energy before you and out of the door. Do not forget to clean the energy off the furniture. As you clean the furniture, you may actually perceive the energy like clouds of dust moving past you.

Conclusion If the room is extremely dirty you may need to repeat the activity. Clean (Waterfall and Scraping). Record your observations in your journal.

EXERCISE 48. GROUP ENERGY RAPPORT

Repetitions Perform this exercise before doing psychic work as a group.

Reference See Exercise 27: Energy Rapport.

Preparation Clean (Waterfall and Scraping). Flower to Bud. Tune to yourself. Sit in the Grounded Position in a circle. Link hands with your partners. You may wish to designate one person to read this exercise aloud so that you all work at the same pace.

Explanation This exercise builds group harmony and facilitates teamwork.

Group Instructions Visualize a wind sweeping around the circle, blowing around you front and back, gathering energy from your bodies and blending it. Direct the wind in a clockwise motion and send it sweeping around the circle several times. As you do this, visualize the disparate energies harmonizing. To aid you, you may wish to visualize many different colours whirling into a rainbow and moving faster and faster until all the colours are spun into clear white light. Drop your partner's hands, halting the circular motion of the energy and absorbing the white light that is now tuned energy. The group is now tuned.

Conclusion Now that you are tuned you are ready to do psychic work as a team.

EXERCISE 49. TESTING THE EFFECTS OF EMOTIONS ON PHYSICAL STRENGTH

Repetitions   Six or more.

Reference   See Exercise 19: Emotions and Physical Strength.

Preparation   Clean (Waterfall and Scraping). Flower to Bud. Perform Exercise 48: Group Energy Rapport. Stand in the Grounded Position.

Explanation   We respond to the emotions emanating from people and carried to us by their energy. These emotions can even affect physical strength. The advantage of performing this exercise in groups of three, rather than with partners, is that the Tester cannot be influenced since he does not know what emotion is being sent. He, therefore, can make no judgement as to whether the Responder 'should' go weak or not. In this way a true test of the physical effects of emotions carried by psychic energy is possible.

Tester's Instructions   Before the experiment begins, do the muscle test on the Responder to determine his baseline strength so that the effects of emotion can be gauged. Then, as the Sender delivers an emotion, you will perform the muscle test on the Responder. Monitor yourself to be sure that you are using the same amount of pressure each time.

Sender's Instructions   Choose a series of five clear, strong, easily distinguishable emotions, and note them down. You should stand at a distance of about five feet from the Responder, preferably where neither of your partners can see you. When you have chosen your emotion and feel it clearly, generate energy and visualize the energy that carries this emotion as flowing from your body and surrounding the Responder like a fog. Notify the Tester when the Responder is completely surrounded by the energy.

Responder's Instructions   Remember to hold the arm that is being tested at a right angle. If your arm goes too far to the side or too far up, or if you clench your fist, additional muscles will be brought into play, and the test will not be accurate. Be sure to resist with the same amount of pressure each time you are tested and to change arms if you become tired. Keep in mind that this is a test of an energy technique, not a test of your strength or that of your partner. It is not necessary to read the emotions. Merely allow yourself to respond. Note down the result of each sending.

Conclusion   Clean (Waterfall and Scraping) and compare notes. Change roles and repeat. Record your observations in your journal.

EXERCISE 50.   GIVING UNTUNED ENERGY

Repetitions   One.

Reference   See Exercise 24: Experiment with Tuned and Untuned Energy.

Preparation   Clean (Waterfall and Scraping). Flower to Bud. Tune to yourself.

Sit in a circle around the Perceiver in the Grounded Position. Do not perform Exercise 48: Group Energy Rapport.

Explanation The purpose of this exercise is to show what happens when a person absorbs a large amount of untuned energy. Exercises 50 and 51, taken together, are an experiment in the differences between the effects of absorbing untuned energy and of absorbing energy that has been tuned to your vibration. You will want to keep this in mind as you perform these exercises. If you do them in separate sessions you should be especially careful to make clear notes.

Senders' Instructions All Senders will work in unison. The Perceiver may read aloud the instructions for generating energy (Exercise 1) so that everyone works at the same pace. Then all Senders give energy simultaneously to the Perceiver. It is important that all Senders remain tuned to themselves throughout this exercise.

Perceiver's Instructions Relax. Breathe deeply. Absorb the energy that your friends give to you, just as you learned to absorb energy from the environment (Exercise 8). When you have absorbed enough energy, pay careful attention to how you feel. Evaluate your body's responses carefully. Do you feel light or heavy? Energetic or listless? Alert or groggy? After you have a clear sense of your responses, send energy to a partner. How strongly can you send it? How well are you able to direct it?

Conclusion Change roles and repeat until every member has taken the Perceiver's role. Tune to yourself. Record your observations in your journal.

EXERCISE 51. GIVING TUNED ENERGY

Repetitions One.

Reference See Exercise 24: Experiment with Tuned and Untuned Energy.

Preparation Clean (Waterfall and Scraping). Flower to Bud. Sit in a circle around the Perceiver in the Grounded Position.

Explanation This exercise illustrates the difference between absorbing tuned and untuned energy.

Senders' Instructions Get a sense of the Perceiver's energy, as you did in Exercise 23, by placing your hands close to his body. Notice his vibration, its frequency and tone. You may even want to visualize it as a colour. Now sense it with your right hands and reproduce the Perceiver's vibration with your left hands. Check it. Does it feel the same? Generate energy. When you feel ready, send energy out from the palms of your hands, tuning the energy as it flows through your palms so that its texture and the Perceiver's vibration match exactly.

Perceiver's Instructions Relax. Breathe deeply. Absorb the energy that your friends give you, just as you did in *the preceding exercise. Once more,* evaluate your body's responses carefully. Send energy to a partner. How strongly can you send it? How well can you direct it? Make notes. Compare with Exercise 50.

Conclusion Change roles and repeat until every member has taken the Perceiver's role. Record your observations in your journal.

Trouble-shooting If the Senders did not tune the energy completely, you will feel uncomfortable. Clean and tune to yourself.

EXERCISE 52. SEEING ENERGY

Repetitions This exercise is done in five-minute sets of no more than thirty minutes' total duration.

Reference See Exercise 32: Seeing Energy.

Preparation Clean the room psychically. Clean (Waterfall and Scraping). Flower to Bud. Sit in a circle in the Grounded Position. Energy is most readily visible against a solid dark background. Darken the room so that only silhouettes are discernible.

Explanation Since a group of people can generate a large amount of energy, and since the energy is of varied frequencies, seeing energy is made easier by working in a group.

Sender's Instructions Generate energy in the centre of your body. Fill your body with light and allow the light to coalesce. You will want to direct energy in various ways. Here are some suggestions.

(a) Send energy out through your fingers towards the ceiling. Spread your fingers, then close them. Do this several times slowly. While you are opening and closing your fingers, project different variations of energy. You may want to go up and down the spectrum or musical scale. Simply changing vibrations will make the energy easier to see.

(b) Direct energy from your right hand to your left through your finger tips. You may also want to move your hands to cause the energy to flow diagonally.

(c) Choose a partner. Both of you should generate energy. Put your fingers four to six inches apart and send concentrated energy to each other. Gradually move your fingers in order to make observation easier.

Perceiver's Instructions The challenge in physically seeing energy is simply learning what to look for. No special effort of the eyes is needed. It is not necessary to stare or strain. When you are successful, you will see white streaks, vapour, or sparks of energy. Some people see colours. Perception will come most easily for you if you are relaxed and performing this exercise in a playful spirit.

Conclusion Change roles and repeat until every member has taken the

Sender's role. Clean (Waterfall and Scraping). Record your observations in your journal.

Trouble-shooting   Keep in mind that our goal is to develop reliable perception; this does not necessarily depend on physical sight. If you are tired after this exercise, you may want to exchange energy with nature.

EXERCISE 53.   EXPERIENCING ENERGY DRAIN

Repetitions   One.

Reference   See Exercise 35. Experiencing Energy Drain.

Preparation   Have the rock salt ready. Clean (Waterfall and Scraping). Takers will sit in the Grounded Position in a circle around the Perceiver.

Explanation   Performing this exercise as a member of a group offers you the opportunity to learn from other people's experiences. It also makes the task easier for the Takers and the experience clearer and more thorough. The purpose of this exercise is to illustrate the experience of energy drain so that you can correctly diagnose it should you experience it in the future. In fact, after consciously experiencing energy drain, your body will react to it very quickly and your defence will be almost a reflex.

Perceiver's Instructions   Lie in a relaxed position on your back with your feet apart and your arms at your sides. Breathe slowly and evenly, and focus your awareness on your energy-body. You may wish to compare your sensations with those you experienced when your partner was taking energy from you in Exercise 2. Keep your friends informed as to your sensations.

Takers' Instructions   Draw energy from the Perceiver using the palms of your hands. Each of you will simultaneously take energy from a different part of the Perceiver's body. You will take from the head last, very gently. You may find it helpful to use a visualization such as iron filings being drawn to a magnet, or coloured liquid pulled through a siphon. Deposit the energy in the rock salt.

Monitor's Instructions   Write down the Perceiver's observations and comments. Should the Perceiver begin to experience dizziness, light-headedness, or severe aches, instruct the Takers to stop draining energy. In any event, the drain should stop in three to four minutes.

Conclusion   Change roles and repeat until all members have taken the Perceiver's role. Record your observations in your journal.

Trouble-shooting   Most people feel tired after energy drain. However, symptoms of energy loss vary, and you may feel dizzy, nauseous, irritable, or depressed. You may be less well co-ordinated than usual. All these symptoms are common and will vanish in a day or two. Allow yourself to experience fully whatever your symptoms are. We have found that the more uncomfortable the experience is, the better your later defence will be. If you still feel tired two days after the energy drain, you may want to perform Exercise 36: Bud to Flower.

From time to time it happens that a person will actually feel better after experiencing energy drain. He may feel more energized and alert. This occurs if his energy-body was very congested and the energy flow was, therefore, impaired. Draining his energy removed the congestion that was impeding the free flow of energy. People who have had this experience will profit from regular practice of Exercise 6: Flowing Energy Through Your Entire Body, and from Exercise 8: Exchanging Energy with Nature, being careful never to draw in more energy than they send out.

EXERCISE 54.   DISCERNING ENERGY DRAIN

Repetitions   Two or more.

Reference   This exercise is not duplicated in the earlier sections because it requires a group.

Preparation   Have the rock salt ready. Clean (Waterfall and Scraping). Flower to Bud.

Explanation   The purpose of this exercise is to train you to discern when you are being drained by someone in your immediate vicinity, as well as to sharpen your psychic perceptions in general.

The challenge of this exercise is to determine which member of the group is taking your energy or is giving energy to you. Each of you will take the Perceiver's role in turn and will leave the room so that the Sender can be designated. You will then be blindfolded and will perceive from which direction the energy is being moved and whether it is flowing to you or from you.

Sender's Instructions   Decide whether you are going to give energy to the Perceiver or take energy from him. If you are giving energy, you will first form a globe of light in the centre of your body. Fill your body with the energy and direct it out of your hands in a steady stream, focusing on one part of the Perceiver's body. Maintain this flow until the Perceiver indicates where he feels energy moving and whether it is being given or taken.

If you are taking energy, you will want to place your hands a few inches from the Perceiver. Visualize the energy in the Perceiver's body as flowing out to fill your hands. Place the energy into the rock salt, and then draw energy again. Do this several times, until the Perceiver indicates whether energy is being given or taken, as well as from what direction the energy is being moved.

Other Group Members   Sit in a circle around the Perceiver. Build an energy barrier between yourself and the Perceiver. Be sure that you are not sending or taking energy inadvertently. Focus on your barrier.

Perceiver's Instructions   Sit in the centre of the circle. Breathe deeply and focus your awareness on your energy-body. Is energy being given to you or being taken from you? Where is the energy flowing?

Conclusion   Change roles and repeat until all members have taken the Perceiver's role. Clean (Waterfall and Scraping). Record your observations in your journal. Compare notes.

EXERCISE 55.   SHIELDING A GROUP

Repetitions   Two or more.

Reference   See Exercise 44: Shielding Another Person.

Preparation   Clean (Waterfall and Scraping). Flower to Bud. Stand in the Grounded Position.

Explanation   This is an exercise that both requires and builds psychic strength; therefore, it should be done after you have attained proficiency in building psychic shields. The group will divide into three parts. One member will take the Defender's role. The others will divide into two groups, the Shielded Group and the Perceiving Group. You will alternate roles.

Defender's Instructions   Visualize a large bubble containing both your group and yourself. Generate energy; visualize the Bubble Shield; direct energy to form it; and solidify the shield. Signal to the Perceivers when you are ready.

Shielded Group's Instructions   Are you comfortable in the shield? Is it large enough? Touch it from within. Is it of uniform thickness? Give the Defender feedback. Make notes.

Perceiving Group's Instructions   Check the shield. Can any of you drain energy from any member of the shielded group? Touch the outer boundary of the shield. Determine its shape. Is it solid? Brittle? Check it for holes.

Conclusion   Dissolve the shield. Change roles and repeat until all members have taken the Defender's role. Clean the room psychically. Clean (Waterfall and Scraping). Record your observations in your journal and compare notes.

EXERCISE 56.   DEFENDING AGAINST GROUP ATTACK

Repetitions   Two or more.

Reference   See Exercise 42: Testing Your Shield with Energy Forms.

Preparation   Clean (Waterfall and Scraping). Flower to Bud. Divide into a Defending and an Attacking Group. Stand in the Grounded Position. Work outdoors if possible.

Explanation   This exercise is an intensive test of your ability to build a strong shield around a group.

Defender's Instructions Make a shield containing the Defending Group and yourself. After the Attackers have tested your shield, dissolve it. When each member of the Defending Group has had his shield tested, exchange roles with the Attackers.

Attacking Group's Instructions Send a barrage of negative energy and energy forms. How well does the Defender's shield withstand it? Check his shield and give him feedback.

Conclusion Change roles and repeat until all members have taken the Defender's role. Clean thoroughly. If you have been working indoors, clean the room. Dissolve any remaining energy forms or place them in the rock salt. If any energy forms penetrate the shield and strike you, you must remove the foreign energy and clean the wounded area. Record your observations in your journal. Compare notes.

Advanced Variation A After the Defender has been successful in shielding his group members against attack, they can test him further. They should talk to him while he is defending against the attacking group. They should try to distract him. How well is he able to maintain the shield?

Advanced Variation B: Defended Group Perform Exercise 48: Group Energy Rapport. Working together, design, visualize, build, and solidify a group shield in unison.

Advanced Variation B: Attacking Group Perform Exercise 48: Group Energy Rapport. Organize and execute an attack as a unit.

APPENDIX

TERMS

Energy-body   The energy-body has a complex structure, similar to the physical body of which it forms a part. It corresponds in shape and size to the physical body and extends approximately an inch outside it. All psychic work is made easier by the proper use of the entire energy-body.

Channels   The paths that energy follows as it flows through the energy-body are termed channels. As you use your energy-body for different tasks, it develops channels suited to those tasks. Just as a weightlifter develops upper body strength and a horseman develops strong legs so you will develop the energy channels that relate to the kinds of psychic work you do most often. Although the channels that have to do with maintaining physical organs are active at all times, the channels that are used for psychic perception activate in response to immediate need and conscious direction. (See also the section on energy channels following Exercise 36.)

Energy-field   The energy-field is the furthest extension of the energy-body and is used when psychic perception takes place at a distance. Like the physical body and the energy-body, it has a complex structure.

Aura   The aura is energy exuded by the energy-body. It follows the general contours of the body and has no discernible structure.

EXPLANATIONS

Natural-Fibre Clothing   Energy can flow freely through fabrics made of natural fibres. You should, therefore, do psychic work in cotton, linen, silk, rayon, or woollen clothing. Energy cannot flow through man-made materials such as plastic, polyester, acrylic, and nylon, which insulate the energy. You should wear these synthetic materials only when you do not want either to send or to receive energy. Such insulating materials should never be worn when you do any exercise in this book. Even the wearing of underclothing of synthetic materials will interfere with the flow of energy. Leather shoes and cotton socks may be worn; bare feet are even better. Since metal collects energy, no jewellery should be worn when doing psychic work. The models in the photographs are wearing leotards only for artistic reasons; you should not work in leotards. The best garb is loose, comfortable cotton clothing.

The Use of Rock Salt Sodium Chloride absorbs and stabilizes energy. Rock salt is a more efficient absorbing medium than other forms of sodium chloride, such as table salt, because the crystals are larger. Since it absorbs energy, salt also absorbs psychic dirt. Rock salt provides a convenient way to stabilize this static energy so that it can be disposed of. It is possible to determine when the rock salt has become too heavily charged to absorb more energy by simply feeling the surface of the salt. If you can discern energy half an inch above the surface of the salt, then it is time to throw it away. Salt with darts or other energy forms in it should always be thrown away.

Because we do not yet know the structure of psychic energy, we can only speculate as to why rock salt acts upon it in this way. The theory is that it may have to do with the molecular and crystalline structure of salt. It is interesting that salt has been considered a cleansing medium for many centuries. Although we do not fully understand why it attracts energy, we can speak with assurance about its effect. As in so many other instances throughout history, the practical application has been learned well in advance of the theoretical knowledge that will provide full understanding.

Cleaning Jewellery Unlike gold and silver, various precious stones, even when cleansed of foreign energy, have their own perceptible vibrations. Diamonds are very difficult to clean psychically because of the peculiar way they retain energy. Students of this book should concentrate their efforts on gold and silver, and on stones that are easier to clean than diamonds.

Psychic Stress The best cure for psychic overwork or overstimulation is physical exercise. When you are doing psychic work, your energy flows through the channels or meridians in your body which govern your psychic perceptions. Maintaining focus on psychic perceptions can cause these channels to become overstimulated. This stress will impair the functioning of your meridians for psychic perception and will impede the development of new meridians. When you focus your attention on some other activity which uses entirely different channels, such as intense physical exercise, your energy moves into the channels which are specific for that activity. This changing of focus allows your energy-body to relax and your channels to return to their normal elasticity.

The Problem of Suggestion Perhaps you doubt your own perceptions. Perhaps you fear that you have been deluding yourself, that you have perceived only because you told yourself you would perceive. It is good to doubt. One grain of honest doubt is worth a bushel of blind belief. And it is perfectly true that the problem of suggestion is real. It is not only real, it is the proverbial two-edged sword cutting both ways: you may suggest yourself into believing something that does not exist, or you may suggest yourself out of perceiving something that does exist.

The only solution to the problem of suggestion is to test your perception. Test it repeatedly. Test it with different people. Test it at different times. Test it under different circumstances.

Someone might say that since he had never perceived psychic energy until he was instructed, his perception is suspect because he was led to it. In fact, this is true of almost everything you learn. Perhaps you have seen a film of primitive people who see a photograph for the first time. They cannot understand it as a depiction of reality. They see it as a piece of paper containing light and shadow, and they look at it with blank, polite smiles. When they are shown how to look at the photo, their perception of reality changes. They recognize people and objects in the photograph. When this happens, the nature of their world has changed. We can only perceive what we can conceive.

Consider music appreciation. You are trained by the society in which you live to hear sounds and patterns and to react to their aesthetic order. If you listen to music from a culture with which you are unfamiliar, you will almost certainly be unable to discern its aesthetic order. You are likely to find it confusing and annoying until you have been taught how to listen. Then you may become a fan. This even happens with Western music from a different time. Are you able to appreciate the music that was popular in the tenth century? Probably not, unless you are a student of music.

Every person's life has many examples of things he was blind to until he was taught. In fact, if we were limited to what we can learn all alone, we would not know much. Nevertheless, it is not the intention of this book to propagandize. We do not want to inspire faith in psychic energy. We want to stimulate its clear-eyed, unbiased study.

Using the Head in Psychic Work There is a tendency to overuse the head for absorbing and sending energy. People do this because they do not fully understand that both absorbing and sending energy are acts that require strength and large channels, whereas the head has many delicate channels used for perception. Additionally, many people tend to over-use these channels simply because the channel's sensitivity makes it easier to perceive that energy is moving. Other parts of the energy body are stronger, however, and more capable of easily and comfortably moving a larger amount of energy and moving it more quickly. It is easier and better to develop some sensitivity in areas which are strong than to try to develop strength in areas which are sensitive. If large amounts of energy are sent through those delicate channels, they will not remain delicate. They will become tougher and less capable of clear perception. In addition, if you *gather a great deal of energy in your head, the delicate channels that* normally direct energy throughout the rest of your body will be too overloaded to function properly.

If you gather too much energy in your head or push a quantity of energy through it, you will become lightheaded. As with alcohol, or drugs, or your first cigarette, the high that occurs from improper use of energy is your body telling you that you are abusing it and that it cannot function correctly.

This is why we emphasize that you should use the whole energy-body, letting the strong parts support the more sensitive areas. In this way, each part functions at its best and according to its nature.

The Use of Drugs The use of alcohol, marijuana, and other mind-altering drugs has a deleterious effect on psychic abilities. Perception and control drop markedly after the absorption of a very small amount of alcohol. Before you have had even enough alcohol to become relaxed, you have had enough to affect your psychic perception. No mind-altering drugs should be used when you are practising psychic skills. Certain drugs, such as LSD, can force psychic centres to open, thereby causing harmful effects that may last for years.

The ability to alter states of consciousness meaningfully is an important skill for those of you who will continue your study beyond this book. This ability should be developed with care so that it can be used effectively and reliably. We strongly recommend that those of you who are serious about developing your psychic aptitudes be very wary of drugs of any kind.

A Word to Psychic Sensitives Psychic sensitives are people who respond more acutely than others to the emotions carried by energy. Often they are not aware of what is happening or that they have an unusual talent. Instead, they are most likely to be confused. Many of the emotions that they experience seem to have no cause and to bear no relationship to anything in their lives. In such cases, they are likely to be actually responding to the emotions of other people. Generally speaking, the emotions most likely to be picked up are the strongly felt but un-expressed emotions of someone to whom the sensitive is close, either emotionally or spatially. Additionally, sensitives may readily internalize other people's opinions and accept these opinions as being their own self-knowledge. Further, they may experience conflicting emotions from a group of people and mistakenly attribute their feelings to internal psychological conflicts. They may even come to doubt their own stability.

In order for sensitives to develop their talent into a usable asset, they must first recognize that they are responding to other people's energy and emotions. Simply realizing that emotions are carried by energy will help. Observing and analysing both their own feelings and their emotional environment will also prove helpful. Learning to distinguish between the emotions that arise within them and those that are transmitted to them is essential. Working with energy, particularly exchanging energy and reading emotions on energy, can be of great assistance in that process. Cleaning and shielding are also very useful. Sensitives should psychically cleanse themselves after all group contacts and should shield when they are in dirty, hostile, or even extremely energized environments. They will find exchanging energy with nature very helpful and should also tune to themselves frequently.

Psychic sensitives have a real and valuable talent. They can relate to others in an authentic way. They will empathize with people's real emotions and are not likely to be misled by what people pretend or mistakenly think they are feeling. Not only that, sensitives can discern how much truth people are able to hear. Their perception makes them the most tactful of friends and confidants. They are readily able to understand group dynamics and the interplay of emotions and influence. Moreover, it is the sensitive who can most readily develop his talent and become an expert reader.

Excess Energy and Energy Drain A person whose channels have been blocked by foreign energy, and a person whose channels have collapsed due to energy drain, will experience similar feelings of fatigue, lethargy, irritability, or depression. The symptoms spring from the same cause in both cases. Often what is experienced as a lack of energy is caused by impaired energy flow. Energy channels cannot function properly when too much energy has been forced through them, whether this is because the person has inadvertently absorbed a mass of foreign energy or because a mass of energy has left his body through energy drain. In either case, the channels have been forced to carry an amount of energy greater than their capacity, and normal energy flow has been impaired.

If you experience these symptoms, assume first that you have been overwhelmed by foreign energy. Clean thoroughly and tune to yourself. If you have absorbed too much energy, these techniques will allow your energy channels to resume their normal functioning, and you will feel better at once. Even if you have been drained, this technique can only be beneficial. If the symptoms do not disappear, then probably you have been drained. Realize that your body will need time to repair itself. If you still feel bad in a day or so, perform Exercise 36: First Aid for Collapsed Channels, followed in six or eight hours by Exercise 6: Flowing Energy Through Your Entire Body. This will allow your energy channels to resume their normal functioning.

The best defence against being either overwhelmed or drained is to build a strong shield. Exercise 35: Experiencing Energy Drain will make your defence almost a reflex. Exercise 54: Discerning Energy Drain will enable you to tell quickly whether you are being drained or not.

Masculine and Feminine Energy-Bodies Masculine and feminine energy-bodies reverse roles with their physical counterparts. The channels in the masculine energy-body and delicate and sensitive, thus orienting it towards work requiring perception and precision. On the other hand, the channels in the feminine energy-body are large and strong, thus orienting it towards tasks requiring power and stamina. As with physical bodies, generalizations are only partial truths and there are many individual differences.

Although the masculine energy-body is by its nature better organized for *perception than the feminine energy-body, conditions in our culture have* operated in such a way as to make the reverse seem true. As is demonstrated in the exercises in this book, too much energy can cause perceptions to shut down. That factor, along with the cultural aspects of masculine development, has caused most men to close off their psychic perceptions at an early age in response to both psychic dirt and psychological propaganda. Thus, the feminine energy-body, which is less affected by random energy, has generally better withstood psychic stress and has not closed off psychic perceptions.

The result is that, generally speaking, men and women need to work on the following aspects. Men need to develop their psychic strength; they need to be constant in practising the calisthenics described in this book. Women need to develop precision and control. They need to work at sending fine beams of energy and at controlled perception. A common occurrence in classes is that during the early exercises women often send too much energy to their masculine partners; the men's channels may shut down and the men then will have little or no perception until they have cleaned and rested for a while.

Both men and women usually have some psychological adjustments to make to their new roles. Men are more accustomed to having power than to having delicate perception. The change of orientation is difficult for them. It is often even more difficult for women. Unlike most men, they have not learned from their youth to be careful with their strength. Also, many women find the experience of being strong so novel and so heady that they use their power carelessly. People should be polite with their energy. Through conscientious practice of the exercises in this book, students will develop both the strength and the reliable perception which are necessary to good psychic work.

THE PSYCHIC STUDIES INSTITUTE

The Psychic Studies Institute offers a uniquely rational approach to psychic instruction. Its goal is to bring psychic skills out of the realm of the supernatural and into the realm of practical discipline.

Psychic skills are part of the natural range of human talents and can be a part of everyday life. With proper coaching, anyone can develop psychic skills and can enjoy their benefits.

The Psychic Studies Institute offers a varied curriculum which develops skills in different psychic areas. The core curriculum consists of fifteen different courses and new courses are added as research develops. Certificates of specialization are offered in Psychic Technology, Energy-body Massage, Reality Creating and Self Transformation, Psychic Self-Defence, and Psychic Reading. Attaining a Certificate takes two to three years.

The Psychic Studies Institute is a tax-exempt, non-profit educational organization, and classes are open to students of all nationalities, races, and creeds. For more information write to the Psychic Studies Institute, P.O. Box 270654, Houston, Texas 77277, USA.

Of further interest

THE MEDITATOR'S MANUAL

A Practical Introduction to the Art of Meditation

If you have always wanted to practice the art of meditation but didn't know how to begin – this book is exactly what you have been looking for. **Simon Court** has devised a completely new approach to meditation. Here, for the first time, his system is explained in full detail. A fully comprehensive programme of exercises and explanations allows you to experience a wide range of meditation techniques for yourself. Through actual experience you can decide which techniques suit you best – and how you can benefit personally from meditation. Contents include:

- carefully structured exercises for experiencing 8 pure types of meditation

- pathworking techniques and fantasy journeys

- 'feedback' sections for assessing the nature of individual experiences

- guidelines for group work

- special tables for personal record keeping

At last the bewildering array of methods and systems has been made crystal clear in this all-embracing manual. From its pages you can create your own path of personal development and embark on a journey of self-discovery.